HERALDS OF A NEW REFORMATION

HERALDS
of a
NEW REFORMATION

THE POOR OF SOUTH AND NORTH AMERICA

Richard Shaull

ORBIS BOOKS

Maryknoll, New York 10545

The Catholic Foreign Mission Society of America (Maryknoll) recruits and trains people for overseas missionary service. Through Orbis Books Maryknoll aims to foster the international dialogue that is essential to mission. The books published, however, reflect the opinions of their authors and are not meant to represent the official position of the society.

Library of Congress Cataloging in Publication Data

Shaull, Millard Richard.
  Heralds of a new reformation.

  Bibliography: p.
  1. Church and the poor—America.   2. Poor—America.
3. Liberation theology.   4. Christian communities—
Catholic Church.   5. Catholic Church—Latin America.
I. Title.
BV639.P6S49   1984   261.8'3456   84-11857
ISBN 0-88344-345-7 (pbk.)

To

Paulo Wright
"disappeared" in a Brazilian prison, 1973
Mauricio López
"disappeared" in Argentina, 1977
Hiber Conteras
imprisoned in Uruguay
and other colleagues
who have paid a high price
for their commitment to the poor.

Contents

Forward, by Paul Lehmann   *ix*

Preface   *xi*

Introduction   *1*
   The Poor and Theology in Latin America   1
   Coming Closer to Home   4
   The Power of a New Message from an Ancient Source   5

Chapter 1
The People of Israel:
The Historical Vocation of Liberated Slaves   *13*
   Rereading the Bible   13
   Israel: An Oppressed People Seeking Liberation   15
   The Source of Israel's Unique Social Vision   17

Chapter 2
The Witness of the Prophets   *23*

Chapter 3
Jesus, the Messiah of the Poor   *39*
   Jesus the Person   39
   A Prophet in Israel   40
   The Prophet as the Messiah   42
   The Kingdom in History   46
   Jesus, Announcing Life, Killed as a Subversive   49
   The Birth of Hope in the Midst of Death   51
   The Liberation of the Poor through the Renunciation
      of Power   54

Chapter 4
When Empires Decline   *58*
   Theology and the Crisis of the Roman Empire   58
   Theology and the Crisis of Empire Today   67

Chapter 5
Looking at the World from Below   *76*

Chapter 6
Changing Values and Changing Sides   *86*
   Changing Values and Lifestyles   86
   The Side of the Poor   94

Chapter 7
A Decent Life for the Poor   *101*
   Toward a New Economic Order in Poor Nations   101
   Toward a New Economic Order in the United States   108

Chapter 8
Basic Christian Communities   *119*
   The Poor and the Bible   122
   A New Form of Community   123
   A New Reformation   125
   A Political Force   126
   A Next Step for Us?   128
   The Process of Liberation in Latin America   134
   The Process of Liberation in the First World   135

Works Cited   *139*

Foreword

Richard Shaull has drawn his considerable and deepening missionary, theological, biblical, and personal commitments and convictions together in this clear, quiet, evocative, challenging, and persuasive report on trying to be a Christian and a citizen of the United States at the same time: *in this time. Heralds of a New Reformation* is to the twentieth century drawing to a close what John Bunyan's *Pilgrim's Progress* was toward the close of the seventeenth century, and still is. There are "the slough of Despond" and "the City set on a Hill." There are the whole armor of faith and the fiery darts of the principalities and powers. But the solitary journey toward the celestial city and the lamentations, weeping, and wailing that surround it have given way—in Shaull's "Pilgrim's Progress"—to the surprises which overtake the faithful when revelation and liberation meet. *Then*—solitariness finds a sustaining companionship, and fear, frustration, and alienation are transfigured in the discovery through the Bible and involvement with the poor that God became human—not so that we might become divine—but so that we might become companions of those most dehumanized by exploitation, oppression, and suffering, and together with them enter upon a fully human life. The celestial city is still before us; but the foretaste of it and the journey toward it are modestly, movingly, and meaningfully described in these pages.

These pages also unmask the self-justifying and polemical disavowal of liberation theology by those who have wittingly or unwittingly surrendered to the self-confidence, the achievements, and the temptations offered by the principalities and powers that have brought "the First World" into being, and keep it going. Shaull displaces their proud and self-confident ideology by a responsible witness of his own to what those who have seen and witnessed who the poor are in "the Third World," and the human future coming to be through them, have said and done. An impressive sequence of citations of the creative theologians of Latin America supports the sobering finding that they are the heralds of a new Reformation. The Protestant Reformation put the Bible into the hands of the people. The new Reformation expresses and exposes what the people found. What the people found was that the Bible "relates to all aspects of life in their world. It describes their struggle in society and helps them articulate their hopes for a more human and just order." Priests and nuns, Catholics and Protestants, Christians and Marxists have come together with the poor in base communities. And there they have discovered that the Gospel, rooted in the Bible, transcends and transfigures ideologies. The discovery is that in the Bible there is "one single Word for one single world."

For those of us in the "First World," living as we do "in a society deeply troubled because it can dream of no future beyond the continuation of what it is now—and is in danger of losing," this book is a timely and renewing account of the vision of the people of the "Third World" and of the new future which their vision can offer to us as well. Here is a primer of Christian discipleship! It is a study book for Christians, isolated in main-line churches, or in the ghettoes of a corporate, financial, and technocratic society, from the transforming power of biblical faith to deliver them from the materialism that destroys human initiative, encourages superficial interpersonal relationships, and diminishes human worth. Congregations and church judicatories who "take time to be holy" will be nurtured by Shaull's report in the imagination, the understanding, and the will to begin to create a more human society. *Heralds of a New Reformation* is an invitation to pilgrimage and hope through which the blind recover their sight, the deaf their hearing; and through which the dead are raised to newness of life (Luke 7:22). Salvation is nearer now than when we first believed (Rom. 13:11).

PAUL LEHMANN
Charles A. Briggs Professor
of Systematic Theology, Emeritus
Union Theological Seminary, New York

Preface

A new Reformation has begun in Latin America, primarily among Roman Catholics. Most of us are aware that it is happening and that poor people are at the center of it. We have heard of priests and nuns who have gone to live with the poor and support their struggle, and we know that quite a number of them have been persecuted or martyred. We have read in the press of the new church of the poor and of the basic ecclesial communities, around which this new church is taking shape. We are most aware of the theology of liberation, denounced by some as Marxist while being heralded by others as the most creative theological movement of our time.

We also sense, quite rightly, that these new developments in the Christian world in Latin America are going to have a significant influence on our life in the First World. The liberation theologians' criticism of capitalist society and the way it affects people and society in Latin America must not be ignored. A high percentage of the men, women, and children being slaughtered in Central America by groups and governments the United States supports are Christians, leaders and members of the base communities. That fact increasingly is going to haunt those of us who live in the United States.

Moreover, there are many poor people in the First World. As their suffering becomes more intense, the life and thought of Latin American Christians may appeal not only to them but also to others who see the injustice of which the poor are victims. And sooner or later those of us in the First World who take the Bible seriously will have to face the fact that the poor and those who stand with them in Latin America are reading it differently and challenging our interpretation of it.

We need to hear what these sisters and brothers in the faith are saying to us; their experience is important for us as well. If we listen to them, we will at first be shocked and perhaps resent their criticism. But if their challenge helps us to understand better what is happening around us and respond more courageously, new vistas will open for us. In Latin America this religious revival has radically transformed many persons' perception of their society and has given them new life and energy as they have taken on the task of changing it. The same thing could happen to us.

There are a number of ways we can expose ourselves to these developments. We in the First World can have firsthand contact with Latin American Christians by traveling to their countries; those of us in the United States can also have that same contact by being open to the increasing numbers of Latin Americans who visit us or live in our midst. Orbis Books, in Maryknoll, New York, has made a tremendous contribution to this dialogue by publishing translations of the most important works of the theologians of liberation.

For some time, however, I have felt that something else was needed: a short volume which introduces the main themes of Latin American liberation theology to readers in the First World and at the same time points out how it relates to their situation. This is the task I have undertaken in these pages. I have taken one central theme, *the poor,* and have attempted to present what various biblical scholars and theologians have to say about it. Then I have looked at some of the implications they have drawn regarding perspective and values, lifestyle and action in society. I have neither done a systematic analysis of the thought of the major theologians nor attempted to identify the points of agreement and disagreement among them. What I have tried to do is to capture the main thrust of their thought as related to specific questions, raise it up in such a way that we in the First World might engage in dialogue with them, and suggest how their thought challenges our understanding of and response to our situation.

In these pages I am concerned to present what the theologians of liberation are saying and to interpret their thought correctly. But I cannot claim to do so with detached objectivity. I speak here as someone who has faced the same human situation they face, who shares their concerns, and who has worked in close collaboration with some of them over the years. I first went to live and work with the poor in Colombia forty years ago. I was so shaken by that experience that I was forced to re-examine all that I believed and was compelled to call attention, within the Protestant community, to the social dimensions of Christian faith. Later, in Brazil and elsewhere, I participated in the formation and development of a movement, Church and Society in Latin America, dedicated to this task. I brought these same concerns with me when I returned to the United States in the midsixties.

In 1978 I was invited to attend a conference of Latin American theologians and social scientists held in San José, Costa Rica. It was there that I became aware of the richness and vitality of the new theology. Shortly thereafter, I had my first contact with the basic ecclesial communities. And then the Reagan administration helped to convince me that what Latin American theologians were saying about poverty and injustice also applied to the First World and to the United States in particular. My decision to leave my post at Princeton Theological Seminary was in part motivated by the desire to spend more time in Latin America, study what was happening in Christian circles there, and find ways to make that thought and experience more available to those in the First World who were becoming interested in it.

Although I have spent three decades teaching in theological seminaries, this book was not written primarily for theologians. I hope that it will be read by pastors and seminary students. However, I primarily intend to speak to women and men who come from a religious background, are concerned about poverty and injustice, but do not have formal theological training. I am especially interested in reaching those who are on the fringes of church life or have left the church because it has not spoken to their deepest social concerns. Some readers from such a background may not find the language used here very appealing. But it is the language being used in Latin America by the theologians and the members of the base communities. I hope that my efforts to use it and at the same time interpret it may make it possible for some to find this adventure stimulating and worthwhile.

Introduction

THE POOR AND THEOLOGY IN LATIN AMERICA

In Latin America the poor and the theology of liberation are intimately related. That theology originated as a response to the sufferings of the poor. Now it plays a major role in orienting and sustaining their struggle. This interaction between the two is, at one and the same time, the consequence of fundamental changes in the situation of the poor and one of the most important factors contributing to an accelerated process of change. In this dynamic and complicated picture, three things stand out.

1. *The great majority of persons in Latin America have always been poor, but now, after three decades of emphasis on "modern economic development," most of them are poorer than before.*

In many rural areas the development of agribusiness, which is oriented primarily toward production for export, has pushed persons off the land and thus deprived them even of the opportunity to grow their own food. For many the only source of income is seasonal work harvesting sugar cane or other crops. Hours are long; wages are low. The poor are often brutally treated and forced to live together in the most inhuman conditions.

Vast numbers of persons drift to the larger cities—an estimated 300,000 arrive each year in São Paulo—where they live completely abandoned in the shantytowns they themselves have built on the outskirts of the city. Those lucky enough to find a regular job may have to travel three or four hours to and from work, and no matter how hard they try, they never seem able to break out of their poverty. The vast influx of persons into the cities combined with the fact that most new industries do not employ large numbers of workers produce very high rates of unemployment.

1

During my more recent travels to various countries, I tried to compare the situation of the poor with what I had seen forty years earlier. In the rural areas, conditions appeared almost identical, except that many families have less to eat today. In urban centers, the shacks now being built in the poor neighborhoods are shabbier, and the rate of unemployment is higher. Then, many persons in the communities I worked in were desperately poor, but I rarely found a household in which no one had any sort of regular work. Many families did not have enough to eat, but they got by. In the poor neighborhoods of the major cities I visited recently, I found many families that depended on soup kitchens to provide them with their only meal of the day.

2. *The poor always knew they were poor; now they know why. They once accepted poverty as their fate; now they know that their suffering is produced by a social order that they can change, and they are determined to change it.*

This change has not been brought about by Marxists. It is the result of both the process of modernization—which has upset the poor's traditional way of life and has opened their eyes to what is happening around them—*and* the participation of the poor in basic Christian communities. In these communities the poor are discovering that they can help each other understand how their society functions and are being provided with the tools they need to undertake this task.

This new knowledge, combined with their desire to improve their lot, leads to the formation of cooperatives and other self-help ventures. It also expresses itself in the organization of and participation in peasant leagues, labor unions, and political movements. When the poor, who constitute the great majority of the population, begin to act politically in this way, they run afoul of military dictatorships. Then repression, arbitrary arrests, and torture are used to control popular movements. When this does not suffice, the army, police, and paramilitary groups kill local leaders and their families. As a peasant from Guatemala said to me recently: "A few years ago any peasant who joined a cooperative or took a course in adult education was considered subversive and might be killed at any moment. Today if you're poor, you're subversive."

3. *The poor and those who stand with them are now taking the initiative in the transformation and renewal of society.*

While the rich and powerful are obsessed with holding on to what they have and go to ever greater lengths to justify their maintenance of the status quo, the poor are taking the lead in articulating a vision of a more human and just future and are demonstrating their willingness to pay the price required to build a new social order.

The immediate goal of the poor is, of course, to improve their lot. But in the midst of that struggle, many of them are discovering that something is more important to them than simply getting a bigger share of the pie. They have begun to dream of a society in which exploitation and oppression can be overcome. At the same time a growing number of women and men who benefit from the present state of affairs are changing sides. They are finding that their lives take on greater meaning as they live in solidarity with the poor and share in their struggle. Out of these joint efforts a new vision for the future of the world is taking shape. It is a vision of a world in which the resources of each nation can be used to provide for the basic needs of all and in which those formerly despised and rejected will have a new sense of their own worth as they participate in the exercise of public power. It is in this milieu that a fire, capable of re-creating the world, is once again being kindled in many souls.

To a surprising extent Christians are involved in this breakthrough. Even in countries in which the church has been thoroughly integrated into the dominant culture and has benefited from its identification with those in power, groups of Christians have broken out of their domestication and are participating in the liberation struggles around them. It is in the basic ecclesial communities that the poor themselves are coming together and discovering that they are persons of worth, that they can work together to solve some of their own problems, and that they can play an important role in the struggle for change. And it is in the church that a growing number of those who are not poor are challenged to share the poor's lot and take up their cause. There seems to be something about the Christian faith that disturbs the conscience of well-to-do persons, breaks out of the limitations set by the institutions it creates, and speaks in a special way to the poor and those who hear their cry.

COMING CLOSER TO HOME

For a long time most of us in the First World have assumed that poverty is a problem of the Third World and that we need not be unduly concerned about it in our own lands. Now we are at least beginning to realize that such is not the case.

The poor are all around us; their number is increasing, and their situation is getting worse. For instance, the economic recession has had its most devastating impact in the United States on those whose situation was already precarious: blacks, Hispanics, women, the elderly, and the rural poor. When our economic system is in crisis, our most immediate reaction is to try to save it by cutting back on those few benefits and services provided for those who have no secure place in it. Thus as unemployment rises, governments cut unemployment benefits, remove large numbers from the welfare rolls, and reduce the funds available for medical care, housing, and legal services for the needy. The recession may end soon, but economic recovery this time may not be accompanied by a sharp reduction in unemployment or a significant improvement in the conditions of the poor and marginalized.

If this happens, we will be forced to recognize that our society is so structured that some can enjoy affluence only if others are deprived of what they need for a decent life. In other words the fundamental problem causing social unrest in Third World countries is built into our society as well.

This conclusion was forced upon me while living in the South Bronx. The Hispanics who live in that section of New York have been dumped there, on the junkheap of our advanced technological society. Because their former subsistence economy in Puerto Rico has been destroyed, they find themselves unemployed and make their way to New York. Large numbers of them cannot find the sort of jobs that would give them a secure place in the economy of the United States, yet their cheap labor is needed to clean office buildings, wash dishes in restaurants, and provide manual labor in the small, illegal sweatshops hidden in the burned-out sections of the Bronx. They are surrounded by affluence, yet they know it is not for them. They live in the United States, in the *First World,* but they have about as much control over their lives and destinies—in the political as well as the economic orders—as the peasants in the hills of Puerto Rico or in the interior of Brazil. And they represent only one of numerous groups in our society that find themselves in the same situation.

Can the same thing that is happening in Latin America happen in the First World? Will the most deprived victims of our system take the lead in challenging the values of our consumer society, developing alternatives to it, and thus opening up possibilities for a more human future for all of us?

I believe they will. I also believe that Christian faith and community will be at the center of such a process of transformation. Religious faith continues to occupy a central place in the life of the poor in the First World. They are in a position to hear the gospel message of liberation, as the poor have done in Latin America, respond to it with conviction, and re-create the early Christians' community of sharing (Acts 2:42–47; 4:32–37). Moreover, a revitalized Christian faith will challenge men and women who are not poor to change sides, and the church can provide an institutional structure within which this can take place. Small groups of priests and nuns, as well as some Protestant communities, have already taken this step, and something similar to the base communities of the poor in Latin America is developing here in the United States. Our contact with the thought and experience of Christians in Latin America could well accelerate this process.

THE POWER OF A NEW MESSAGE
FROM AN ANCIENT SOURCE

Many of us in the First World are keenly interested in the theology of liberation as it has been developed in Latin America. But some of us, when we begin to study it, have serious problems with it. I would like to refer briefly here to two reactions that have arisen frequently in courses and discussions that I have been a part of here in the United States.

1. These theologians present us with a different perspective

from which to reinterpret the Christian story as a whole. Biblical scholars call this a hermeneutical principle. As the theologians of liberation have read the Bible and have explored the heritage of faith in the context of the suffering and struggles of the poor, they have been grasped by a new and compelling message: God is acting redemptively in history to liberate the oppressed. This has become a new paradigm that orients their work. Its power is demonstrated by the richness of thought it is producing, its appeal to many who are deeply concerned about the suffering and injustice around them, and, above all, by the fact that it serves to articulate the faith by which the church of the poor in Latin America is now living.

At the same time we are compelled to ask, Is this a correct interpretation of the gospel message, or are the Latin Americans reading into it what they want to find there? As we struggle with this question, we should, I believe, keep a couple of things in mind.

Christians who try to make sense of their faith and articulate it in a coherent way must accept the risks involved in making use of a hermeneutical principle. Both the Old and the New Testaments contain a number of literary forms and a rich variety of images, symbols, and perspectives. The biblical story can speak to us only as we immerse ourselves in its richness and think about its meaning in relation to our specific human situation. Each New Testament writer did precisely that, and thus we have in it a variety of interpretations of the meaning of the life, death, and resurrection of Jesus Christ. Across the centuries the same thing has happened again and again.

In fact, I would claim that Christian faith has had the power to transform human life and thought because it has been capable of re-creating itself again and again. When we read the Bible with new questions in our minds and in a new historical situation, we should expect it to speak a new Word to us. We should assume that we will find a new message that may have been there waiting for us all the time. After it has broken through to us, we can only say, How is it that I never saw it before? In the words of the German-American historian and social philosopher Eugen Rosenstock-Huessy, "the Gospel is always the Good News of tomorrow, never the Good News of yesterday."

Martin Luther, in the midst of a profound crisis—his own and that of his age—rediscovered and rearticulated the Pauline doctrine of justification by faith. He then proceeded to reinterpret the Bible and theological tradition in the light of that principle. John Calvin did the same thing with his emphasis on the sovereignty of God. Through these and many other such efforts, our understanding of the gospel has been enriched and expanded.

We go to the Bible with our questions, concerns, and prejudices. Thus we always run the risk of finding and choosing only that which confirms and supports what we already think. But if we are open and honest with ourselves, something else happens. We go to it determined to interpret it in line with our own perceptions and perspectives, and we end up allowing this Word to interpret us and our world. Because of this turn of events, a new vision often emerges, hope is rekindled, and life is enriched.

Standing in the line of Christian reformers, the Latin American theologians of liberation dare to offer us, in our present situation, a new principle for the interpretation of the gospel of human redemption. If it shocks us, that may be all the more reason for us to take it seriously or at least to question our reasons for rejecting it. If we cannot agree with what they are saying, that does not necessarily mean that they are wrong. It may rather expose the limitations of our own perspective. As long as we judge every new hermeneutical principle by those we have inherited from the past, we violate the gospel itself and condemn ourselves to stagnation. New interpretations of the faith, in response to new situations, can only be evaluated adequately by the development of new criteria.

In these situations we are called upon to use all our critical faculties at the same time that we are open to surprises and to the possibility that we may be mistaken even when we are most sure of ourselves. We are free to do this if we realize that the truth of any new interpretation of the Christian message will ultimately be demonstrated, not by reason alone, but by history. When a new vision of what Jesus Christ means for the world commends itself to us, we will test it out in the light of what the Bible has to say, and we will make use of our reason to examine it critically. But we will also live it out, and in doing so, perhaps over several generations, we will test its validity and perceive its limitations.

2. If some reject the theology of liberation because it has departed from tradition as they know it, others turn away from it for the opposite reason: it seems to rely too much on traditional language and categories. Most of the systematic theologians involved in this movement have spent years studying the Western theological tradition. They now reinterpret it, to be sure, but they do so making use not only of traditional theological categories but of the type of language and conceptual thought that goes with them.

Does this language have the power to illumine our human situation today and orient us in it? Many of us find it to be quite alien to our thought and experience. We become even more skeptical when we see how this language is being used by those who want to continue living in the past, to shore up values and structures now being called into question.

At times, however, we may suspect that this heritage has a much greater influence over us than we are willing to admit. Ernst Bloch, the Marxist philosopher from Germany who gave so much attention in his thought and writings to biblical language and symbols, once remarked:

> Certain aspects of Christianity . . . seem paradoxically familiar to the emancipated man. He seems to meet them anew and encounter their binding force afresh rather than merely remember them as a constant feature of the past [Bloch 1972, 236].

We meet these elements of our heritage "anew" and "encounter their binding force" because they are part of us; they belong to our *social autobiography*. The Christian tradition is not a dead letter enclosed in theological formulae and passed on to us only as we master them conceptually. It is a living and dynamic social reality passed on from one generation to another in the dynamics of human relationships, through the family and the culture as a whole.

I find that I respond to events around me very much as a Calvinist. That heritage has come to shape decisively my attitude toward the world and my sense of what is important in my life.

How did this happen? To be sure, my mother taught me the Shorter Catechism, and I attended Sunday school and church regularly as a child. But family, church, and community, by being what they had become over generations, made that heritage live in me. Later on, my academic study of Calvinism helped me to re-create the faith I had inherited, draw on it as a valuable resource for living, and understand better who I was.

A religious tradition lives in us. It continues to remain alive as it re-creates itself in response to new human situations. It becomes sclerotic and dies when the faith responses worked out in a previous historical situation are reified into dogma and made an object of belief. Consequently, I may learn more about that heritage when I examine *how* it has functioned in previous eras to orient thought and sustain life than when I concentrate my attention on mastering the theological formulations used to express these faith responses.

All this makes an immense difference in the way I, as a Christian, approach the problem of the poor today. I don't start out as a neutral human being looking at a biblical text as an object to be analyzed and discussed academically. I'm a person very much disturbed by the poor persons around me. I know that this is due to the way my father lived, to what happened to me in church, and to the impact biblical stories have made on me. I take up the Bible and read theology in order to understand better why I feel this way and how I can act responsibly. As I examine one or another of these texts, I am especially concerned to see if a new dialogue can break out between my story and the stories they tell—a dialogue that can deepen my self-understanding, broaden my horizons, and motivate my actions.

In the Bible concern about the poor is related directly to God: in the Old Testament, Yahweh, the God of Israel; in the New Testament, God whom Jesus addressed as Father. This God is supremely concerned about the poor, acts in history to liberate them from oppression, and calls those who believe in God to take the cause of the poor upon themselves. If we think of our heritage of faith as our social autobiography, then it would only seem natural that, for us, concern for the poor and faith in God would be intimately related.

Unfortunately, this is not always the case. For many women and men today, including those from a Christian background, traditional language about God has become highly problematical; in fact it often gets in the way of our relating to and drawing on our religious heritage.

Those who react in this way have quite good reasons to do so. The church and many Christians across the centuries have failed to take seriously what the Bible says about the poor. Much of our conceptual thought has transformed God into an almighty power who rules over and diminishes persons. Many men and women who are afraid of risking life as an adventure in growth, love, and service worship a God who provides them with security and represents absolute authority. Those who enjoy the greatest wealth and privileges, as well as those who yearn for them, often worship a God who affirms and sacralizes the world they have created.

This, of course, is not the whole picture. Often those who speak of the absence of God yearn for an experience of transcendence. They are all too aware of how easily their world can become narrow and enclosed, how their sensitivity to other persons can be lost. They have seen how quickly the greatest ideals of justice and equality can become idols and be used as weapons to perpetuate injustice. Nowhere is this more evident than among those persons in Marxist societies who are most concerned about human well-being and freedom.

How then can we explore a tradition which gives such crucial importance to language about God and at the same time so abuses it? I propose that we accept the tradition as part of our social autobiography, in the realization that it is in this language that it speaks to us about who we have been and has provided us with categories for thinking about our humanity and our destiny. We cannot hope to understand ourselves without paying attention to what that language is saying, but our discourse about these things need not be limited to or bound by it. And this dialogue with our past—and with ourselves—need not be reserved for those who can declare that this language about God makes sense to them or that they "believe" it.

Whatever our position toward God, we are all related to and in some sense responding to a common history. The fact that our language about God has become so idolatrous means that those of us who find it meaningful need to be challenged constantly by those who reject it. And those of us who can no longer use this language may discover that our investigation of how it functioned in the past can help us on our journey today.

Chapter 1

The People of Israel: The Historical Vocation of Liberated Slaves

The poor are the only legitimate interpreters of the biblical text, since that text belongs to the historical memory of the poor. The poor are the human authors of the Bible. The entire Bible has been produced by the poor or from the perspective of the poor, which allows them and only them to provide the key to its interpretation. In this sense, the Bible has an extraordinary historical and human originality. In the history of humanity, the dominant groups are usually those who write history. The poor rarely have the possibility of writing their history or of writing it from their perspective. Even when they succeed in doing it, that literature is usually "lost" or destroyed by the intellectual castes serving those in power. In the history of literature, the Bible is an exception: being a book of the poor or written from their perspective, it has survived across the centuries.

Pablo Richard

REREADING THE BIBLE

When we come to realize that the various elements in our cultural and religious heritage have contributed to making us who we are and are thus a part of us, we are faced with a strange paradox: no part of our tradition has a more central place in our history than the Bible, and yet, for those of us who are white, middle-class Christians in the First World, the biblical story stands in the sharpest contrast to our own. Elements of the Bible's message have permeated our cultures and shaped our families and communities; it is communicated to a large segment of each new generation through the concerted educational efforts of the church. But the Bible tells the story of a poor and oppressed people and looks at life and history from that people's perspective; our story is that of nations that have become rich and powerful and look at the world from that vantage point. The experience of blacks in the United States or of migrant Hispanic farm workers is similar to that of the Israelites or of those who gathered around Jesus of Nazareth; ours is not. Can we do anything to bridge the gap and thus be in a better position to hear what the Bible has to say?

If we look at our Christian history with this question in mind, one thing stands out clearly: time and again the biblical Word has broken through with power to men and women in new and difficult situations. For instance, as Karl Barth observed what was happening around him toward the end of the First World War, he came to the conclusion that the culture of the West as well as its major institutions were in a profound state of crisis. In his wrestling with the problem, he took a new look at the Western theological tradition and discovered what he called "the strange new world of the Bible." He found, to his surprise, that this ancient text not only spoke directly to the human situation as he had come to know it but also radically altered his perspective and opened up new depths of understanding of human nature and destiny. But this strange new world was not perceived by everyone who read the Bible. By and large the satisfied participants in and defenders of the "old world" did not see it. Only those who sensed that an era was ending and were searching anxiously for new directions seemed to hear what the Bible had to say.

Today something similar is happening among the poor and those who stand with them. For many of them the Bible opens up a strange new world. As they read it they realize that it is *their* story. It illumines their struggle, sharpens their vision, and sustains their hope for a better life.

In Latin America a growing number of women and men who

are not poor are finding that the Bible speaks a new and compelling Word to them as well. But they are able to hear it only as they enter into the world of the poor, share their suffering, struggle in some way, and allow themselves to be taught by them. Perhaps that experience can be ours as well, if we dare to follow the same path.

Here I can only report on what has been happening to me as a result of my very limited contact with the poor. Reading the Bible now, I find that so many things I had never seen before stand out in bold relief, and a book which was gradually losing its appeal for me is once again exciting reading. Moreover it speaks directly to my troubled conscience and offers me new options for dealing with it. I find myself taking a new look at who I am and who I can become in the light of my own Christian history.

In dealing here with the Old Testament and in later chapters with the New Testament, I am neither interested in nor capable of undertaking a thorough academic investigation. My goal is a much more limited one: to present some of the things I am discovering in my dialogue with the Bible and with the poor and those who stand with them. You may or may not agree with my conclusions; you may or may not find them valid. My hope is that in presenting them I can encourage you to go further in your own exploration of the strange new world awaiting us as we read the Bible with the poor and from their perspective.

ISRAEL: AN OPPRESSED PEOPLE SEEKING LIBERATION

We need no special illumination to see that the Old Testament tells the story of the anguish and struggle of a poor and oppressed people. Other nations of the ancient Near East had gods who stood on the side of the rich and powerful and provided a religious validation for the established order of domination. But the God of Israel called Abraham and his family to abandon their home in Mesopotamia, one of the great centers of civilization and geopolitical power of that time, and become "wanderers." And while this God promises Abraham that his descendants will eventually become a great nation, the immediate prospects are quite different: "God spoke to this effect, that his posterity would be aliens in a land belonging to others, who would enslave them and ill-treat them four hundred years'' (Acts 7:6). The exodus from Egypt is portrayed not only as the central event in the formation of Israel as a nation but also as the key for these persons' interpretation of the meaning of their existence as a people and of their religious faith. But the exodus is the story of the liberation of slaves who were sorely oppressed, "broken in spirit," and facing the possibility of extermination through forced labor projects and infanticide.

For a relatively brief period of time, the Israelites enjoyed national independence, eventually with their own kings. Even then the ethical norms laid down for them in their sacred writings exhorted them to keep alive the memory of their former existence as slaves. This memory was to so shape their national life that they would never fail to care for the widow, the orphan, and the foreigner within their gates (see Exod. 22:21–24; Deut. 15:12–15).

In the seventh century their national life was disrupted by invading armies that carried away one group after another into foreign lands. Eventually some of them or their descendants returned to rebuild Jerusalem and reconstitute their national life. But they never again regained full national independence, being subjected to the rule of one foreign power after another until the time of Christ. A people that traced its origin to a slave revolt in Egypt also knew six hundred years of oppression in the land in which it had established itself as a nation.

We need not go to Latin America to find Old Testament scholars whose studies lay before us these dimensions of the history of Israel. Much research has focused on the exodus narratives and on the influence of this event on the religious thought and life of the people of Israel. Since 1938 Gerhard von Rad has been calling the attention of the Christian world to the exodus story as the creative center of the literature of Israel and of its confessions of faith. He has shown how the three great narratives of the Pentateuch present three readings of the exodus event from three different historical situations. His work, along with that of other scholars, leads us to one conclusion: *In the Old Testament the normative revelation of God occurs in the historical liberation of a people from slavery.* In other words, the God of Israel's self and purpose for this chosen people and for the world were revealed in this event. Consequently this people's struggle for liberation and the approach to life and the world emerging from it should have been the primary factor in the shaping of ethical norms, religious life, and national development. And to the extent that this revelation is considered normative for the Christian community today, the same should hold true for us. Unfortunately thus far these historical studies and their implications for our theology and ethics have had little effect on our spiritual life, our preaching, or the witness of the church.

THE SOURCE OF ISRAEL'S UNIQUE SOCIAL VISION

Further insight into the origin and history of the people of Israel is now being provided by a group of Old Testament scholars who are making use of methodologies and perspectives drawn from anthropology and sociology in order to understand the social structure of Israel. They are engaged in a study of the religion of Israel as a social phenomenon; they are also giving specific attention to the structures of political domination, social stratification, and economic exploitation as they existed in Israel and in the great empires of the ancient New East. The major work produced thus far in this field is Norman R. Gottwald's *The Tribes of Yahweh.* His research is so thorough and the thesis he develops has such radical implications for our interpretation of the Old Testament that I want to summarize his argument at some length. As I understand it, his thesis, based on his studies of the history of the Near East from 1250 to 1050 B.C. and of the historical material provided by the Old Testament itself, is this: *In Canaan the people and the religion of Israel emerged while marginal groups that had revolted against the dominant feudal system came together and struggled to create an antiauthoritarian and egalitarian society.*

This hierarchically ordered feudal system was firmly entrenched throughout Canaan. The pharaohs of Egypt controlled most of the territory with the collaboration of local dynasts. These dynasts, in turn, ruled their city-states with the help of a small aristocracy, based in the urban centers, that exploited the land and the persons under its control. The system was essentially a network of economic, social, and political dependencies. It served the interests of these various ruling groups but left the great majority of the population, especially in the rural areas, bitterly oppressed, economically exploited, and politically powerless. In their number were included not only the poorest peasants but also the serfs, formerly free persons who had lost the few advantages they once enjoyed.

This system produced a large, marginalized underclass composed of peasants, pastoral nomads, and the *'apiru*—bands of outlaws and mercenaries made up of former slaves and priests, thieves, and other deprived fugitives from the dominant order. According to Gottwald these diverse groups of marginalized persons gradually coalesced and revolted against their oppressors. In spite of the fierce opposition of kings, feudal landlords, merchants, priests, and armies, they succeeded in carving out their own liberated zones in the more isolated areas and undertook the construction of a radically different social order.

Their efforts were greatly strengthened by a small group of invaders from the desert, the women and men of the exodus from Egypt. Sustained by a religion celebrating their actual deliverance from sociopolitical bondage and drawing on what they had learned from their years of wandering in the desert, they made a rich contribution to this struggle: a vision of a new society and the energy to create it, skills in social organization, and trained cadres who could provide strong intellectual and political leadership. As the Levites were scattered through all the tribes, these resources were made available to all, and the groups making up the original coalition were more closely united.

The result of all this was the emergence of the people of Israel as a new society. This people had succeeded in cracking open the highly centralized and stratified social order around it and was engaged in the establishment, in contrast to that social order, of a community dedicated to the pursuit of social equality and justice:

> The people who came to be Israelites countered what they experienced as the systematic aggression of centralized society by a concrete, coordinated, symbolically unified, social-revolutionary action of aggressive self-defense. Appropriating the land and economic modes of production, this body of people organized its production, distribution,

and consumption along essentially egalitarian lines. The specific historic rise of old Israel was thus a conscious improvisational reversion to egalitarian social organization that displaced hierarchic social organization over a large area previously either directly or indirectly dominated by Canaanite centralization and stratification for centuries [Gottwald 1979, 326].

This antihierarchical social order had as its foundation large extended families that were free from the obligation to pay tribute to overlords and thus enjoyed a high degree of economic autonomy. These families were united in larger associations; a number of such associations of families combined to form a tribe, and the tribes were bound together in a confederation. Consequently all persons were included in the body politic, and power was widely diffused in society. The tendency of local chiefs to become aggressive and extend their power was fiercely resisted, and checks were developed to the accumulation of economic surplus and the concentration of power in strong families.

For Gottwald this reconstruction of the early history of Israel enables us to arrive at a new and richer understanding of the religion of Israel. It developed in the midst of this social struggle and in direct relation to it. At the same time it was a powerful force that sustained and shaped this struggle decisively. Yahweh was the God not of those on top but of the underclass that was fighting for liberation from oppression. Yahweh willed the creation of a society in which suffering would be alleviated and the exploitation of the poor would be overcome. And the God of Israel's will so transcended even the highest achievements of a new social order that it represented a constant pressure for social transformation.

Yahweh was a jealous God who stood alone, and this God's purpose for the world did not change. Thus faith in Yahweh served to pull together a disinherited people and bind it closely in the pursuit of a common goal. Yahweh's sovereign rule not only defended Israel against external enemies but also served as a bulwark against the abuse of power within Israel itself. Yahweh alone ruled; there was no place for repressive human authority. Belief in Yahweh's consistency of purpose and rule over the future gave the people of Israel confidence that its unique way of life, threatened on every side, could indeed prevail.

Gottwald claims that the religion of Yahweh was quite unique, but "Yahweh's uniqueness lay in the fact that 'he' was the symbol of a single-minded pursuit of an egalitarian tribal social system" (p. 693). He also states,

> As far as I have been able to determine, the high gods of the ancient Near East apart from Yahweh are always adjuncts of politicized societies. Ideas of gods have everywhere come to terms with centralized governments and with social stratification; accordingly, the gods are supramudane authenticators of the political and social order in which a minority of the members of the society dominate the majority. Only in the case of earliest Israel do we have a clearly articulated "national," i.e., culturally comprehensive, religious system wherein the interpreters of the deity do not recognize a central government or the division of society into privileged and nonprivileged strata [p. 689].

From beginning to end Gottwald's study focuses on the development of the religion of Israel as a social phenomenon. His research lays before us a fascinating picture of what may have been the origin of this strange Judeo-Christian history in which our own lives and culture are set. If the main lines of his interpretation of what happened in that distant past are correct, we have here some new clues for solving the riddle not only of where we have come from but also of who we are as a religious people and who we can become.

In addition, Gottwald makes it possible for us to see more clearly the richness of language and imagery that developed in early Israel around what he calls "the exodus-conquest paradigms" that have had a "capacity to give symbolic meaning to a broad range of historic experiences of liberation" (p. 698). Gottwald finds this to have been true especially during the time when the diverse social groups in Canaan came together to form the people of Israel. But these religious symbols continued to manifest their power in the later history of Israel, as is more dramatically demonstrated by the prophets and, from time to time, in the

Christian community among those engaged in a similar struggle to break the bonds of oppression and exploitation and create a society of greater equality and justice. Historical studies of this sort increase the chances that this language will contribute significantly to our struggle as well, as these symbols are illumined by the re-creation of their historical context and, at the same time, liberated from their use and abuse for other ends.

For us as Christians the history of Israel is *our* history as well. That fact raises some further questions for us about the significance of this reconstruction of the origin of the people of Israel. For we belong to a historical community of faith that looks at the history of Israel in a special way. It affirms that, in this particular history, revelation has taken place. In other words, the emergence of the religion of Israel is something more than a creation of oppressed persons in Canaan struggling for liberation. It took shape as persons who were engaged in this struggle felt themselves to be addressed by a voice from beyond and responded to it. As they articulated their faith in Yahweh who validated and sustained their struggle to create a new society, they were also describing an encounter with mystery, a vision they had been "given" of human life and destiny, and a claim that had been laid upon them.

When we approach the history of Israel from this perspective, which has had such a central place in our religious heritage, the implications of what Gottwald has to say may be quite disturbing for us. Theologians have emphasized the fact that the God of the Bible is revealed in the particularity of human history: among the Jewish people in Palestine in the midst of concrete historical events. But if Gottwald is right, then this particularity must be defined more sharply: this revelation takes place in the struggle of poor and exploited persons to overcome oppression and create a society in which all can share and participate. God appears in history as the One who stands with the poor and against those who work injustice. The revelation of God occurs when the poor are raised up and liberated; God's power is manifest in the welding of a marginalized people into a new nation called to live out this vision and carry out this specific redemptive mission in the world.

This bringing together of revelation and liberation will seem very strange to many of us. For some, concerned about the social struggle, the whole idea of being addressed by God no longer makes any sense; others, who often speak glibly about a transcendent God, refuse to even consider what these and other historical studies are telling us about the God of the Bible.

In contrast to this, something quite extraordinary has been happening in Latin America. A number of Old Testament scholars are coming to conclusions similar to those of Gottwald about the history and religion of Israel; their research highlights the centrality of God's concern—as manifested in the Pentateuch and the Historical Books, the Psalms, and the Prophets—for the poor and that justice be done to them. At the same time many of the poor and others who share their struggle are finding that the story of the people of Israel speaks directly to them in their struggles; their experience confirms what the scholars are saying and is beginning to transform and enrich Old Testament scholarship. In addition to this, the poor and those who struggle with them are beginning—in their new community life and in the suffering and martyrdom which often accompanies their struggle—to speak in a new and compelling way about God.

I consider their witness to be a challenge to all of us. It suggests that any breakthrough in dealing with oppression will come not primarily as the result of academic discussions but as the consequence of a new involvement with the poor. It also underlines the importance of maintaining a stance of radical openness: openness to surprises of transcendence and openness to the revolutionary dimensions of the biblical story.

Chapter 2

The Witness of the Prophets

The people of Israel worshiped a God who had liberated it from slavery and who had been revealed in the midst of this struggle. As the chosen people of Yahweh, the vocation of Israel was so to structure all aspects of its life that this liberation of the poor and despised could become a historical reality and thus serve as a light to the gentile world as well. Faithfulness to Yahweh meant constant vigilance to protect this experiment in human relationships from all threats to it, both internal and external. At the same time, efforts to preserve the purity of the faith in Yahweh against all temptations to worship other gods were seen as essential to the maintenance of the unity of this people as well as its radical social vision.

Gradually, however, Israel abandoned its calling. It decided that, as a nation, it also should have kings ruling over it. With the establishment of kingship came greater centralization of power in the hierarchy. As the economy expanded, some groups grew wealthy at the expense of others, and the divine command to care for the poor, especially the orphan and the widow, was forgotten. This fundamental change in society was accompanied by an equally radical change in the religious realm. Yahweh, the liberator of slaves and defender of the poor, was worshiped by the wealthy and powerful, who were able to be at ease in Zion because they considered this God to be on their side. And the religious leaders of the time proved to be quite adept at reinterpreting their religious heritage to serve the ends of the privileged classes.

As Israel departed more and more from Yahweh's order of justice and at the same time faced a series of internal crises as well as repeated attacks from the armies of neighboring empires, a second, historically unprecedented development took place: the emergence of the prophets. From the eighth to the sixth centuries a succession of largely isolated individuals, most of them from the lower classes, dared to reaffirm the earlier vision of a people dedicated to the pursuit of justice and equality. From this perspective they challenged and condemned the established order and predicted its imminent collapse. Speaking out of their heritage of faith and what they declared was a direct encounter with Yahweh, they laid the foundation for what we today would call a counterculture. Their criticism of the existing order cut to the heart of it; they proposed, as an alternative, a society based on justice to the poor, and they dreamed of a new utopian era to be established in the future in radical discontinuity with the social order they confronted.

These men were bitterly attacked and often severely persecuted. Their prophecies were ignored, their warnings unheeded. And yet their oracles have been preserved and occupy a central place in the Old Testament. From there they have become a part of our history as well. As Davie Napier has said, the prophets and their oracles are "ancient Israel's most notable development" and its "most widely appropriated legacy to us and the world" (Napier 1981, 148).

What does it mean for us to receive this legacy, to recognize these men as part of our own history instead of engaging in a detached analysis of their words? As I read the prophetic writings once again, taking into account the exegetical work of Latin American scholars and others, several things stand out in bold relief.

1. *The prophets emerged in a time of national crisis and gained public attention because of their interpretation of it. In the Old Testament they are presented to us as the only ones who, in their time, understood what was happening. But few of us would consider turning to persons like them for guidance in a similar situation of crisis, much less think of following their example.*

They were, first of all, *outsiders*. Most of them belonged to the lower classes, Amos the shepherd of Tekoa being the most notable example. They did not arise in the cities or large towns but more on the periphery; several of them refer to the rural villages, at some distance from Jerusalem, from which they came. They did not occupy important positions in society or in the religious institutions. Amos, for one, declared that he does not even belong to the guild of the prophets. They pronounced God's judgment upon the nations yet showed an extraordinary sense of identification with the poor in their tragedy and suffering. Micah speaks of standing "barefoot and naked" among them. J. Severino Croatto, an Argentinian scholar, describes their stance in these terms:

> The prophets place themselves *in confrontation with* the power structure, and almost always from within the community or the people. The prophets are never from among power elite; they rise from the grassroots or, at least, speak on the basis of their identification with these bottommost strata. Even when they criticize *the people* of Israel, they do not do so as power-holders but by using the single weapon of their word [Croatto 1981, 40].

These prophets dared to confront the wealthy and powerful and declared that the historical development of their nation had turned out to be one great failure. And in the midst of the struggle they were caught up in, they demonstrated an amazing sense of personal freedom and individuality.

Micah declares that the recognized religious leaders who announce that all is well shall be disgraced and that he is filled with authority, justice, and might to denounce the transgressions of Israel (3:8). Jeremiah states that he is set over nations and kingdoms to pluck them up and break them down (1:10). Their boldness was the result of one thing alone: an inescapable call from Yahweh. Their response to this call meant a radical break with their past life. As von Rad puts it, "it was a totally new way of life . . . to the extent that a call meant relinquishing normal social life and all the social and economic securities which this offered" (von Rad 1965, 58). They were overwhelmed with a great burden yet completely isolated. Says Jeremiah: "I did not sit in the company of merrymakers, nor did I rejoice; I sat alone, because thy hand was upon me" (15:17). They had little or no hope of success; as a result of their preaching, those in power hardened their hearts and thus brought on disaster more quickly. The prophets themselves suffered ridicule and persecution, and the lives of some of them, as in the case of Jeremiah, were repeatedly threatened.

In the midst of all this, these socially insignificant people became the incarnation of a new quality of human life. Responding to an external compulsion, they were unusually free in their personal lives and in their relationships with others. In the words of von Rad, "Just because he [the prophet] has received this call he is able to enjoy an entirely new kind of freedom" and establish a "unique kind of converse with men" (p. 76). They not only challenged the kings and princes of their time; they also complained to and argued with Yahweh and at times refused to obey Yahweh's directives to them. They often add their own explanations to the "Oracle of the Lord" and dared to issue their prophecies in their own names, which was something very new at that time. They speak out of an experience that had transformed their consciousness, intensified their mental capacities, and led them to express themselves in daring new poetical forms.

Most disturbing of all, these countercultural rebels turned out to have been, by and large, right in their reading of history. Their powerful attacks on the established order of their time have come down to us while the cautious and optimistic statements of religious and secular leaders have long since been forgotten. Moreover, the religious community that refused to listen to them nevertheless decided to honor their memory and preserve their prophecies as part of its sacred literature.

All of this, I believe, poses a number of questions for us. Whose voices are we inclined to listen to in a time of crisis? Should we give more importance to those who stand outside of the structures of power or to those properly-behaved men and women within the system? To whom do we turn in search of vision or to catch a glimpse of hope for the future? Especially within the church, given the fact that the prophets and their witness belong to us, these questions must continue to haunt us. It may be hoped that our concern about them will help to create a little space here and there in which such people can emerge and find each other, speak out, and be heard.

2. *The prophets were supremely concerned about one issue: social justice*. Latin American exegetes and theologians are clearing away the ideological underbrush that has kept us from seeing this with greater clarity, and they are challenging us to deal with its implications.

Taking the lead in this effort is José Porfirio Miranda, a Mexican scripture scholar. After having studied economics and theology in Germany, he returned to Mexico and became involved with poor industrial workers. As he began to look at the world through their eyes and to study the writings of Karl Marx, he found himself reading the Bible from a different perspective and discovering in it things which his professors had never taught him. He went back to Europe and spent several years doing exegetical work in both the Old and New Testaments. These studies confirmed his suspicion that Western scholars, with all the tools at their disposal for analyzing the biblical texts and for understanding the historical situation in which they were written, were often unable to see some of the central elements in the biblical story.

Returning once again to his work with the poor in Mexico, Miranda continued his research and wrote several books, two of them being *Marx and the Bible* and *Being and the Messiah*. These volumes are not easy reading, but they merit careful study on our part. We may not agree with all of his conclusions, but the richness and depth of his thought can challenge us to undertake a careful reexamination of what the various biblical writers are saying. Here I would like to point out some of the ways in which Miranda has changed my own perception of what the prophets have to say.

I had assumed for a long time that justice was the central theme of the prophets. I didn't realize, however, how this concern pervades their thought or how often it has been obscured by translation and by exegetical comment. For me the prophets represented the incarnation of a *passion* for justice. I now see that, whatever their subjective feelings on the matter, the heart of their message is this: social justice should be the foundation on which each nation is built. The creation of a just social order is the raison d'être of nations and local communities, of social structures and institutions. This applies especially to Israel. Its existence as a nation is the consequence of a successful struggle for liberation. More than that, it is bound to Yahweh by a covenant, a mandate to establish justice and thus be a light to all the nations of the world (see Isa. 42:5-7).

I learned years ago that in the Old Testament justice means something quite different from "giving to each their due," as the Greeks conceived of it. Miranda sharpens this distinction in a number of ways. He declares that for the prophets justice includes restitution. Injustice is spoken of in very concrete terms: it refers to the way the poor are deceived by judges who have been bribed or merchants who use false measures; to the peasants whose little piece of land has been taken from them; to the situation of those who are hungry or victims of violence and persecution.

In other words, *the test of justice is what happens to the poor*, to those who have nothing, are powerless, and have no one to defend them. This is the burden of the prophets. Time and again they described—whether in the brusque and dramatic phrases of Amos and Micah or the polished poetic language of Isaiah and Jeremiah—the rich and powerful and their treatment of the poor:

Hear this, you who trample upon the needy,
    and bring the poor of the land to an end,
saying, "When will the new moon be over,
    that we may sell grain?
And the sabbath,
    that we may offer wheat for sale,
that we may make the ephah small and the shekel great,
    and deal deceitfully with false balances,
that we may buy the poor for silver
    and the needy for a pair of sandals?" [Amos 8:4-6]

You . . . who eat the flesh of my people.
    and flay their skin from off them,
and break their bones in pieces,
    and chop them up like meat in a kettle,
    like flesh in a caldron [Micah 3:3]

    Your hands are full of blood. . . .
Seek justice,
    correct oppression;
defend the fatherless,
    plead for the widow [Isa. 1:15, 17]

The Lord enters into judgment
  with the elders and the princes of his people:
"It is you who have devoured the vineyard,
  the spoil of the poor is in your houses.
What do you mean by crushing my people,
  by grinding the face of the poor?'' [Isa. 3:14–15].

We could pile text upon text and undertake the exegesis of pas-
sages from one prophet and another in the hope of grasping more
clearly what they say about justice and the poor. These efforts are
essential, but our failure to hear what they are saying may be the
result of something else: a mindset which limits or blocks our
perception. This is the claim Miranda makes. For him it is the
"mental system" at the heart of Western culture that must be held
responsible for our blindness:

> In the Western mental system there is no room for the much
> considered "social justice." . . . In the Western theologico-
> philosophical system, . . . the social problem is new. I can-
> not sufficiently emphasize this fact. Derived from Plato and
> Aristotle, Western culture—whose generative epicenter was
> and continues to be the "Christian" theology-philosophy—
> has been inevitably aristocratic, privileged, incapable of
> perceiving the most massive, tragic, and urgent reality of
> our history. Its humanism was and is a humanism of
> thought—a mental, aesthetical humanism. And its "man"
> is an abstraction, a Platonic essence valid *semper et pro
> semper*, not real flesh-and-blood humanity, a humanity of
> blood and tears and slavery and humiliations and jail and
> hunger and untold sufferings [Miranda 1974, 31].

3. *The prophets lived in times of national crisis. Their interpretation of these crises as well as the solutions they proposed were
considered offensive by their contemporaries. They were denounced as traitors to their country, and their lives were frequently threatened.*
For them the problems of Israel were a consequence of its
failure to live up to its historical vocation: to be a society in which
justice reigned and the cause of the poor and powerless was up-
permost. Consequently, although the prophets speak continually

of social and economic conditions, they show little concern for concrete solutions to economic problems. They discuss the situation of their nation in relation to the powerful empires surrounding it but give little attention to military preparedness, except to say, on numerous occasions, that it will be of no avail. They passionately denounce disobedience to the divine law but not in individualistic terms. As von Rad remarks in his discussion of Amos, "At one fell swoop not individuals but the whole of Israel—or at least her leading men—were sharply accused of flagrant breaches of the law. This was something entirely new" (p. 136). For them there is only one road to national salvation: the re-creation of a social order in which the poor, the marginal, the fatherless, and the widow will have a chance for a full human life.

If Israel fails to choose the path of justice, then its destruction as a nation is certain. In the words of Hans Walter Wolff, the burden of Micah's prophecy is that "those who trample justice under foot in God's city will experience God's doom in the city they first plundered for themselves" (Wolff 1981, 131). Time and again one after another of the prophets repeats this refrain. And as they fill in the picture of the doom awaiting a nation no longer dedicated to its historical mission of justice to the poor, they come to two daring conclusions. They declare that the fate of not only Israel but of all the nations surrounding it will be determined by this same criterion. At the same time they insist that Israel's failure to live up to its vision will lead to even greater destruction, precisely because this vision was Israel's special vocation in history.

The prophets are well aware that nations in crisis are not likely to turn to prophecy or visions for their salvation. But they state categorically that reliance on wealth or military power will achieve nothing. Only the pursuit of justice can save those nations:

> Let not the wise man glory in his wisdom, let not the mighty man glory in his might, let not the rich man glory in his riches; but let him who glories glory in this, that he understands and knows me, that I am the Lord who practice steadfast love, justice, and righteousness in the earth [Jer. 9:23-24].

Those who put their trust in anything else will be confounded. In the midst of their pride and sense of grandeur, they will know failure and defeat. And their humiliation is often described in dramatic terms, as when Isaiah speaks of the great nation of Egypt in a state of utter confusion, staggering as a drunken man in his vomit (19:14).

From the perspective of the prophets, the pursuit of justice in history is more important than the survival of a nation or its institutions. In fact social disintegration and national defeat are seen as necessary steps toward the creation of a more just society and are therefore affirmed. Jeremiah is called "to pluck up and to break down, to destroy and to overthrow, to build and to plant" (1:10). Micah sees Zion plowed as a field, the holy city of Jerusalem a heap of ruins (3:12). And Isaiah speaks of Yahweh "smiting and healing" Egypt as well as Israel (19:22). Only after Jerusalem has been reduced to ruins will it become the center from which peace and the Word of God will flow. Israel will be wounded, taken into captivity in Babylon, and after that raised up. Only as Zion is stripped of its power can it serve God once again as an instrument of peace.

In other words, *the prophets introduce radical discontinuity as an important positive factor in historical development.* Without it, justice for the poor cannot be achieved in a society structured to the advantage of the wealthy and powerful. For Davie Napier this represents the radical new element in the message of the prophets of the eighth century. Up to that time even the prophetic voices in Israel were concerned about building a people and a culture in continuity with the past; they saw the future of the nation as an extension of what had been, the result of a process of evolutionary development. The classical prophets, however, envisage "discontinuity between the present and future, the catastrophic imposition from without of disorder and chaos, the abrupt and violent termination of Israel past and present" (p. 168).

Religious leaders in other cultures of that time counted on their gods to save their nations, and those in power in Israel often did the same. The prophets not only separate Yahweh from the survival of the nation—declaring that Yahweh, the God of justice, measures the people with a plumb line and destroys what is out of line—but they go so far as to declare that Yahweh can destroy what Yahweh created.

It is at this point that the prophetic understanding of history stands in sharpest conflict not only with the perspective of the conservative defenders of the established order but with that of liberal reformers as well. And two thousand years of Christian influence has done litte to change all this. In fact, by and large, the church, except on rare occasions, has ignored this vision and has tended to incorporate what the prophets denounced most vigorously. Marx and Marxist movements, not Christian theologians and the church, have been responsible for giving a contemporary expression to this prophetic insight and working out its implications for our time. And contemporary attacks on Marxism often go far beyond a rational critique of its failings; they express the deep resentment, on the part of those who profit most from the status quo, against any perspective which suggests discontinuity. For them survival is the ultimate value.

In Latin America today, as Christians begin once again to speak this prophetic word and live out this vision that justice for the poor can come only as the present order is overcome, they too are becoming the victims of intense hatred. In fact the number of martyrs in recent years suggests that when Christians recover this element of their heritage they may be more exposed to attack and persecution than those identified with Marxist movements.

4. *In the midst of the destruction of their nation, brought on by its failure to fulfil its historical vocation, the prophets introduced a new and powerful force into history*: messianic vision.

They began to dream of a new era of peace and justice more radical and more utopian than anything in their history. So intense was their passion for justice for the poor and so strong their faith in Yahweh's action in history to establish such an order, that they affirmed that the suffering and defeat of the people of Israel would be the occasion for a new beginning. Its defeat would open the way for a new historical action on the part of Yahweh to achieve the end for which the nation was created. Thus they speak of a new exodus, a new David, a new entrance into a new land. There is rich diversity in their visions of the new age and in their understanding of how it would come about. Some speak of a relative degree of institutional continuity with the past; others affirm a completely new beginning. Some expect the new order to be established by a new King David; others put their hope in a remnant gathered from among the humble and despised who, like the dew, are unobtrusive and yet effective. In Deutero-Isaiah we find the striking image of the suffering servant.

From their descriptions of the future messianic age, two themes emerge with particular power. Firstly, their vision of a new order is one in which the marginalized, those who are the victims of hunger, oppression, and fear, will enjoy a full and safe life:

> I will rejoice in Jerusalem,
>   and be glad in my people;
> no more shall be heard in it the sound of weeping
>   and the cry of distress.
> No more shall there be in it
>   an infant that lives but a few days,
>   or an old man who does not fill out his days.
> For the child shall die a hundred years old,
>   and the sinner a hundred years old shall be accursed.
> They shall build houses and inhabit them;
>   they shall plant vineyards and eat their fruit.
> They shall not build and another inhabit;
>   they shall not plant and another eat;
> for like the days of a tree shall the days of my people be,
>   and my chosen shall long enjoy the work of their hands
>   [Isa. 65:19–22].

> And the trees of the field shall yield their fruit, and the earth shall yield its increase, and they shall be secure in their land; and they shall know that I am the Lord, when I break the bars of their yoke and deliver them from the hand of those who enslaved them. . . . They shall dwell securely, and none shall make them afraid. And I will provide for them prosperous plantations so that they shall no more be consumed with hunger in the land, and no longer suffer the reproach of the nations [Ezek. 34:27–29].

Secondly, the messianic age will be a time of peace, but it will be peace with justice, the peace that comes when oppression has been overcome. It will be a time in which swords will be beaten into plowshares and spears into pruning hooks; "the wolf shall dwell with the lamb and the leopard shall lie down with the kid" (Isa. 11:6). The social revolution undertaken in Israel will not only triumph there but will spread around the world. All the families of the earth shall be blessed, for "in days to come Jacob shall take root, Israel shall blossom and put forth shoots, and fill the whole earth with fruit" (Isa. 27:6).

With the appearance of messianic vision came also a fundamental shift in the perception of time. Attention is directed toward the future; the iron grip of the past over society is broken. If the real Israel, the land where the poor are liberated and justice and peace reign, is still to be created, if it will come about as the result of decisive future events, then those expected events become the center of attention. Men and women begin to look at what is happening around them in the light of the new order yet to be established. To the extent that this happens, old institutions lose some of their legitimacy; past achievements, no matter how great, are relativized, and the human spirit is set free to dream and to live expectantly.

Many centuries have passed since this breakthrough first occurred; the words of the prophets have become part of the sacred canon of the Western world; in some circles we now speak rather glibly about eschatology and the possibility of allowing the future to set the terms for the present. Yet how rare it is, even today, to find individuals or communities, to say nothing of nations, who dare to dream of new alternatives rather than living in bondage to the exhausted options of the past.

For those of us who are Christians, the challenge is a double one: to cultivate a messianic vision capable of shaping our understanding of our own societies *and* to take seriously the responsibility of building communities of faith in which the fragile dreams of the poor and powerless can be nourished and sustained. In times of social disintegration, the future of our nations rests in the frail hands of those women and men who, as their cherished way of life is collapsing, do not despair, because they are beginning to envision a richer life and a more human social order that will come only through the radical transformation of what we now have.

The tired defenders of the status quo, who have wealth, prestige, and power on their side, will fight for nothing more important than their survival. Only those who now possess nothing more than a dream can offer us life in the future. The church, when true to itself, is the place where those who carry this burden for an entire generation can meet each other, be affirmed vis-à-vis the dominant culture, and find strength to continue the struggle in the face of repression and persecution.

5. *Latin American theologians have uncovered another central theme running through the prophetic writings*: To know God is to practice justice to the poor.

Jeremiah puts it this way:

> Woe to him who builds his house by unrighteousness,
>   and his upper rooms by injustice;
> who makes his neighbor serve him for nothing,
>   and does not give him his wages;
> who says, "I will build myself a great house
>   with spacious upper rooms,"
> and cuts out windows for it,
>   paneling it with cedar,
>   and painting it with vermilion.
> Do you think you are a king
>   because you compete in cedar?
> Did not your father eat and drink
>   and do justice and righteousness?
>   Then it was well with him.
> He judged the cause of the poor and needy;
>   then it was well.
> Is not this to know me?
>   says the Lord [22:13–16].

Nothing could stand in sharper contrast to modern religiosity than this. Our most intimate relationship with God is highly individualistic. It would hardly occur to us that we should seek God in and through our relationships with other persons, much less in and through relationships with the poor, broken, and marginalized women and men around us. In evangelical Protestantism we speak of finding God in a highly charged emotional experience; in both Catholic and Protestant circles our language about God is grounded in Greek conceptualizations. God exists for us as we develop the right concepts. God's being is worked out as these concepts are rationally related to each other. In this way God is objectified and can be talked about with intellectual detachment; even ethical issues can be discussed quite objectively as rational deductions from first principles.

The prophets, speaking to their contemporaries, called anything like this idolatry: these gods were human creations existing only in the minds and hearts of those who had invented them to serve their own ends.

If we today yearn for an experience of transcendence, if, to use St. Augustine's words, our hearts are restless until they find rest in God, then we might consider the prophetic way: to open our lives to the poor and take their struggle for justice upon ourselves. As we do this we may find ourselves called and transformed. In this sharing of life with the outcasts and dispossessed, we may have unexpected experiences of grace and joy, of vitality and strength, of hope and trust. And, as we find new life in the midst of their suffering, we will realize that an inescapable imperative is laid upon us.

Some decades ago a number of European theologians, following Kierkegaard, placed great stress on the complete otherness of God. For them the abyss between the human and the divine was bridged only by God's self-revelation. Latin American theologians also speak of otherness but give their own special perspective of it and concreteness to it: We can understand and experience the other only as we open ourselves to the poor and respond to the call mediated to us through them. In the words of José Miranda:

> Only the summons of the poor person, the widow, the orphan, the alien, the crippled constitutes true otherness. Only this summons, accepted and heeded, makes us transcend the sameness and original solitude of the self; only in this summons do we find the transcendence in which God consists. Only this summons provides a reason for rebellion against the masters and the gods in charge of this world, those committed to what has been and what is [1977, 37].

God's self-revelation can never be expressed authentically in abstract thought about God, human life, and the world. It is first of all a call, mediated in and through the poor, to men and women in the past and to us; in response to it we discover who we are and what human life is destined to become. In this situation of involvement, as we use our mental powers to reflect upon our predecessors' and our own experience, we can hope to grasp what God offers us and thus develop intellectual resources of value to us in our journeys toward personal and social liberation.

Scientific analysis and historical research are indispensable resources for these journeys, but problems arise when the assumptions on which these means of inquiry are based, as well as the methodologies used by them, are taken for granted as the appropriate ones for theological reflection. That reflection must be, first of all, rooted in the poor. It is not surprising that people in the base communities and those who work with them often reveal a depth of insight and richness of understanding in their reflections on the Bible which are often lacking in more academic studies and discussions.

Latin American liberation theology's interpretation of the words and actions of the prophets reveal several valuable conclusions for us today. Firstly, those of us for whom faith in God and an experience of the divine are important face serious challenges: to take more seriously what the prophets have to say about knowing God in relation to the poor and their struggle for justice; to put their witness to the test and see if it leads to a more vital faith and a richer spirituality. If we are reluctant to take these steps, we must face the possibility that we are guilty of what the prophets most condemn: worshiping an idol of our own creation and finding false security in it.

Secondly, for those of us who are not particularly "religious" and yet find ourselves shaped by and drawing upon a heritage of faith, the insight of the prophets can provide us with a new and different perspective on our situation. We no longer need to think that something may be wrong with us if we can't speak confidently about religious experiences or use traditional language about God. Nor do we have to try to justify our concern for justice within the church. And we certainly are freed from any compulsion to seek satisfaction in types of religious experiences we know to be inauthentic for us.

Thirdly, the challenge before us in the midst of the struggle for justice is to be fully open to manifestations of transcendence in our midst and to the language, images, and symbols that can help break open our world that is constantly in danger of becoming closed. As we do this in a new dialogue with our heritage, we may experience a greater richness of life, hope in the midst of despair, and manifestations of grace which take us by surprise. If this happens, we will know that we are once again living the reality of transcendence, whether we can name it or not.

Finally, along this road we may recover something else that the prophets proclaimed: that God will *become* our God as we struggle for and move toward greater justice for the poor. Miranda emphasizes this point in his discussion of the text in Jeremiah about the new covenant that Yahweh will establish with the chosen people:

> The heart of the matter is that men will not have Yahweh as their God unless they love their neighbor and achieve justice completely on the earth. God will not be God until then. The God whom we claim to affirm when we prescind from the realization of justice is simply an idol, not the true God. The true God is not; he will be [1974, 294].

If we accept this we need neither to spend our energies trying to prove God's existence nor despair of God's absence. It will suffice for us to try to be faithful to the call we have already heard and live in the expectation of a new epiphany.

Chapter 3

Jesus, the Messiah of the Poor

JESUS THE PERSON

Jesus of Nazareth is so much a part of our history and our culture that we treat him like a distant cousin, taken for granted and largely ignored. Certainly, born-again Christians are excited about their personal experience of Christ and, in their excitement, witness to the mysterious appeal of his person across the centuries. At the same time that appeal is at least in part a result of the fact that the carpenter of Nazareth has been transformed in the United States into a "superstar," the object of near idolatrous worship by those who are seeking divine validation for their threatened values and a way out of their frustrated search for personal fulfillment.

In this situation it is hardly surprising that Jesus has come to play a minor role in the lives of many of us who call ourselves Christians. We no longer read the Gospels expecting them to open up an exciting new world to us. Nor do we assume that his Word will transform our lives or help us to interpret what is happening around us.

On the other hand, those Latin Americans who are involved in the struggle of the poor and look at Jesus from that perspective are discovering a person many of them had not known before. They feel a strange new attraction to him and are responding to a call to discipleship, which is having a profound influence on their perception of the world and the direction of their lives. In this chapter I want to present some of the things that these Latin Americans are saying, together with my own comments on their possible meaning for us.

I realize, from the start, that there is one fundamental difference between their approach and ours. They start out as poor people bringing their sufferings and their struggles for liberation to their reading of the Gospels. Or if they are not poor, they have chosen to share the lives of the poor and join their struggle. As these two groups join hands, they find themselves viciously attacked by those in power and often face imprisonment and martyrdom. Few of us in the First World are in a similar situation, and we can hardly imagine what it would be like. Even so we can listen to their witness, and perhaps even be changed by it.

Latin American theologians are giving central importance to the *person* of Jesus: how he lived, what he said, what he did. (See, for example, Leonardo Boff's *Jesus Christ Liberator*.) I propose here to follow their lead. *Who* is Jesus? I believe that the theological question about Jesus is posed most authentically for us when we find ourselves confronted by a person whose words and actions disturb us at the same time that they open new horizons for our life and thought. In the Synoptic Gospels, Jesus raises this question for his disciples only after they have heard him announce that a new age has begun, seen him demonstrate its presence in their midst, and obeyed his command to go out to "preach the kingdom of God and to heal" (Luke 9:2).

By adopting this approach, I am not trying to draw the old line between the Jesus of history and the Christ of faith and focus more on the first than on the second. By now we are all aware that the only Jesus we know is presented to us by men and women of faith and that it is faith in this person as the Christ that has played such an important role in shaping our history and our destiny. I would only contend that we not allow any problems we may have with the traditional christological doctrines to get in the way of a new adventure in response to his person.

A PROPHET IN ISRAEL

Jesus was viewed as living the life of a prophet by the people. Matthew and Mark may go beyond that to designate

> *him as Messiah and Son of God, but that does not invalidate*
> *the historical process of which he is clearly a part. Jesus*
> *transcends prophecy, but from within the prophetic tradi-*
> *tion. This is of incalculable importance. It is in and through*
> *the prophetic dimension that the people and Jesus' disciples*
> *move toward an understanding of who and what Jesus is in*
> *his ultimate reality. Hence one cannot grasp the ultimate*
> *reality of his life apart from his life as a prophet.*
>
> Ignacio Ellacuría, *Freedom Made Flesh*

Jesus of Nazareth belongs to Israel—a nation which, as we saw earlier, traced its origins to a slave rebellion; a people whose God was revealed in the midst of that struggle; a nation with a special historical vocation to do justice to the poor; a nation denounced by the prophets—and later destroyed—for having departed from that vocation; a people that had lived for six hundred years under foreign domination and was yearning desperately for liberation from bondage.

Moreover, Jesus clearly situated himself in the line of the prophets of Israel. When he inaugurated his mission in Nazareth, he applied to himself the definition that Isaiah had given of the prophet and the prophet's task. On several occasions he drew on the prophetic writings to support what he was saying. His life and thought evoked, among the people of Israel, the image of the prophet, and they often spoke of him using this term. At the time of his triumphal entry into Jerusalem, the crowds hailed him as "the prophet Jesus from Nazareth of Galilee" (Matt. 21:11) while the priests and Pharisees hesitated to take action against him at that moment because they realized that the multitudes held him to be a prophet (Matt. 21:46).

Jesus never accepted the title of king except when crowned with thorns; he never called himself a priest except when offering himself in sacrifice. Yet he never refused to be known as a prophet. In fact, at a time when the great prophetic tradition had died out in Israel, Jesus not only reestablished the prophetic role but gave priority to it.

Like many of the prophets he came from the lower classes. The accounts of his birth emphasize his humble origins. His family came from the "hill country of Judea" (Luke 1:65); he was born in a stable because his parents could not afford a room in the inn. His birth was announced only to shepherds in the fields, and he spent his early years working as a carpenter.

When Jesus began his public ministry, he chose to identify himself with the grassroots groups that had no power and were completely outside of the major institutions and centers of power in Israel. He himself was poor, with no place to lay his head, and he spent his time with the sick and lowly, with sinners and foreigners. Most of those around him suffered from the lack of something: food, money, health, prospects, special abilities, prestige in the eyes of the righteous and the rich. From the beginning he addressed himself to the marginalized people.

By taking upon himself the mantle of the prophets, he declared himself to be an outsider passionately committed to the cause of social justice. We may ignore this; his contemporaries did not. For he attracted Zealots as his disciples: members of a movement fiercely opposed to Roman domination and engaged in religious and political resistance to foreign oppression. According to New Testament scholar Oscar Cullmann, not only "Simon the Zealot" belonged to that group, but others like Judas Iscariot and Peter probably belonged and the sons of Zebedee possibly belonged to it. Moreover, by taking a prophetic stance vis-à-vis the established order, Jesus brought down on himself the same sort of hostility and persecution the prophets experienced. He ended up on the cross, condemned to death as a subversive.

If we hope to break out of our ideological bondage and engage in an authentic dialogue with this person, then we need to enter imaginatively into this world and, as best we can, stand where he stood.

THE PROPHET AS THE MESSIAH

And he came to Nazareth, where he had been brought up; and went to the synagogue, as his custom was, on the sabbath day. And he stood up to read; and there was given to him the book of the prophet Isaiah. He opened the book and found the place where it was written,
"The Spirit of the Lord is upon me,
because he has anointed me to preach good news to the poor.

He has sent me to proclaim release to the captives
and recovering of sight to the blind,
to set at liberty those who are oppressed,
to proclaim the acceptable year of the Lord."
And he closed the book. . . . And he began to say to
them, "Today this scripture has been fulfilled in your
hearing."
When they heard this, all in the synagogue were filled with
wrath. And they rose up and put him out of the city, and led
him to the brow of the hill on which their city was built, that
they might throw him down headlong.

Luke 4:16–21, 28–29

During the darkest hours in the history of Israel, the prophets dreamed of a future messianic age, a time when justice would be done to the poor and peace, which comes with the elimination of oppression, would reign. Jesus took up this theme and gave it a central place in his preaching; he drew on the messianic imagery to interpret who he was and what he was doing. At the same time his interpretation of the messianic age carried him beyond the prophets and stood in shocking contrast to the expectations of his contemporaries.

For Jesus the messianic age implied turning the established order upside down. This is most clearly stated in the Gospel of Luke. It begins with Mary's declaration that with the coming of the Messiah God "has scattered the proud in the imagination of their hearts, he has put down the mighty from their thrones, and exalted those of low degree; he has filled the hungry with good things, and the rich he has sent empty away" (1:51–53). The section presenting the core of Jesus' teaching begins with the Beatitudes. They announce that the poor are the lucky ones; the kingdom belongs to them rather than the rich, who already have their reward. Those who are starving will have plenty to eat while those who are full will go hungry; men and women who are having a good time will know pain and tears while those who are crying because of their own suffering and that of others will rejoice. Those who are faithful to the prophetic witness and are hated and persecuted will be richly rewarded while the preachers and teachers of religion who are spoken well of—those who misread what is happening around them and offer religious security to those who practice injustice—will be likened to the false prophets (6:20–26).

Jesus declared that the messianic age had already dawned and allowed himself to be identified as the Messiah. His preaching brought good news to the poor, whose situation would soon change dramatically, and his words communicated the excitement that went with such an announcement. He taught his followers to live *as if* this new age had already begun—to love their enemies, do good to those who hated them, and share everything with those in need, expecting nothing in return (6:27–36). And when John the Baptist sent his disciples to inquire whether Jesus really was the "expected one," Jesus called attention to what he was doing as providing signs that the new age had arrived: "The blind receive their sight, the lame walk, lepers are cleansed, and the deaf hear, the dead are raised up, the poor have good news preached to them" (7:22). The established order was already approaching its end; the process of liberating those who were oppressed had begun.

At the same time Jesus refused to do what was expected of the Messiah: as the agent of Yahweh, imbued with divine power, to overthrow the oppressors and raise up those underneath. He saw this as a temptation to be avoided at all cost; in order to establish the messianic kingdom he would not rely on great material achievements, bedazzle human beings with charismatic appeal, or use the power and glory of the state to impose a new order (Luke 4:1–13). When Peter confessed that Jesus was the Messiah, Jesus immediately spoke about the suffering and death that awaited him. And as he moved toward it, he identified himself more and more with the suffering servant of Isaiah: the liberator of the oppressed who takes upon himself the two things which most characterize the life of the poor, suffering and servanthood.

Jesus' interpretation of the messianic age and of his role as the Messiah profoundly affected his teaching, led to his death, and has left his followers to this day with a number of unresolved problems. Before going into these matters, however, I think it is important for us to pay attention to a question being raised by theologians and members of the base communities in Latin America: How many Christians in North America and Western Europe take seriously what they are saying when they profess faith in Jesus as the Christ? The word *Christ* means *Messiah*. To accept Jesus as the Messiah means to realize that the hour has come for justice to be done to the downtrodden and exploited human beings of the world and thus to admit that the end is near for a social order which provides a minority with rich rewards at the expense of so many others.

José Miranda claims that this problem arose in the church even in New Testament times. In his exegesis of the First Letter of John, he arrives at the conclusion that when the apostle denounces all those who do not accept Jesus as the Messiah and identifies them with the Antichrist, he is speaking about men and women who are members of the community of believers. The problem arises, says Miranda, because anyone who really confesses that Jesus is the Messiah is declaring a supreme concern for a worldwide order of love and justice. But how many Christians live this out? For Miranda,

> The fact that Christians have not set out to conquer the world for love of neighbor shows that they do not believe that the messianic *eschaton* has arrived. . . . By this very fact they deny that Jesus is the Messiah. They have withdrawn from the otherness of millions of hungry, tormented human beings, and they worship a mental idol invented by civilization itself [Miranda 1977, 196].

I would like to carry Miranda's argument one step further. The failure of Christians to live what they profess makes it extremely difficult for those who do hunger and thirst for justice to believe that the messianic age has begun and thus to expect fundamental changes to occur in society.

I think of two close friends, now in retirement. The creation of a more just society has been the major driving force in their lives. Because of this passion, they were attracted to Marxism in their youth and spent a number of years working with labor unions and political movements. Eventually they became disillusioned, and after a number of painful personal experiences, withdrew from those organizations. Some years later they were harassed and put out of their positions in the public school system because of their earlier associations. But in and through it all, they continued to do what they could to work for change. Whenever we get together, they are intensely interested in discussing the international situation and the peace movement, the economic crisis in the United States and elsewhere, the problems of young people, and other social issues. But underlying all of our conversations is one burning question: Can we really believe that social transformation is possible? They want very much to believe it, but they know of no community to which they can turn whose witness might keep their hope alive.

THE KINGDOM IN HISTORY

According to the declaration Jesus makes about the Kingdom of the Father, God has decided to intervene in this world to change it by liberating it from everything that is oppressive: pain, divisions, sin, death. . . . He announces that, with him, this liberating purpose of God is now present. To give concreteness to the love of the Father, Christ begins by associating himself with sinners and other marginalized people of his time. He breaks through the social stratification of that epoch, relativizes the absolute value of religious observances, and claims that privileged access to the Father comes through service to the poor, in whom God is hidden anonymously. . . . Justice occupies a central place in his preaching. He sees poverty as the fruit of unjust relations among people, and declares that the poor are blessed because their existence brings about the intervention of the messianic king, whose mission it is to do justice to the poor and defend the weak. He also speaks out against wealth . . . because he realizes that it is acquired by exploiting the poor. . . . The arrival of the Kingdom implies a break with the established order and the gradual construction of a completely new order in the fullness of time.

Miguel Concha

For some time, New Testament scholars in Europe and North America have been saying that the central theme of Jesus' preaching was the kingdom of God. But the Latin Americans are the ones who have brought this to the fore and have worked out the implications of it for our reading of the Gospels. Drawing on the work of the French and German scholars, they show us what the image of the kingdom meant to those who heard Jesus preach. In the ancient Near East, the king was seen as the one who could ensure justice to his subjects. Those subjects included the rich and the powerful, the weak and the poor. And as the rich and powerful always managed to oppress and exploit the weak and the poor, the king's supreme task was to restore the balance. He was seen as the protector of the widow and the orphan, the poor and the oppressed.

In this context the preaching of Jesus about the kingdom filled the hearts of the poor with joy and aroused great expectations among them. He announced that *this* kingdom was near at hand, that it belonged to the poor, and that their situation would thus change dramatically. In the words of Joachim Jeremias, the distinguished German exegete, "the reign of God belongs *to the poor alone.* . . . The first Beatitude means that salvation is destined *only* for beggars and sinners" (Jeremias 1971, 116). The rich can also enter the kingdom but only through the eye of the needle, only by making restitution to the poor and oppressed and sharing with them in order to be in tune with the new age that is coming.

Jesus not only preached; he also acted. And he claimed that his actions were *signs* of the approaching kingdom. All these actions had to do with bringing health, forgiveness, and full life to the lowest and most marginalized. He touched and healed lepers, who had been banished from the city and cut off from all normal human contacts. He associated with and offered salvation to prostitutes and tax collectors—the moral outcasts in Israel. He cast out demons and accepted those who were demented into his inner circle and called upon the poor and uneducated to be the bearers of good news.

For Jesus all this represented something radically new. It was like new wine that could be contained only in new wineskins. It called for such a profound change in human relationships that it broke the power of old institutions and freed those who responded to him from undue concern about or bondage to them. The kingdom brought with it such a rich promise of new life that no sacrifice was too great to attain it; it was the treasure hidden in the field or the pearl of great price to be acquired even if it meant selling everything. Thus Jesus could ask his followers to give up even family and employment in order to be part of it. Most significant of all, this new era was already breaking into history, and thus those who yearned most for it could see signs of it and expect to see very soon new possibilities for life for the poor and humiliated.

Through this type of exegetical work on those texts in the Synoptic Gospels that have to do with the kingdom of God, the theologians of liberation have made two important contributions to our understanding of the message of Jesus.

Firstly, they call into question any attempt to emphasize the spiritual while ignoring the material side of life or to separate personal salvation from social redemption. The new life Jesus offers is the fullness of personal existence within a transformed society. Salvation is liberation—liberation from all that oppresses and destroys us as persons living in community. Consequently, Gustavo Gutiérrez is justified in saying that "the Gospel does not get its political dimension from one or another particular option, but from the very nucleus of its message" (Gutiérrez 1973, 231).

Secondly, the Latin Americans call our attention to the fact that both the Old and New Testaments deal with God's action and with human existence *in history*. The kingdom of God takes shape on earth. This not only leads us to speak about our faith in historical rather than metaphysical terms, but it also has serious social and political implications for Christians. As Samuel Silva puts it:

> When the future on earth takes the place of the Hellenistic heaven, then the promises of happiness, of participation in the sharing of material things, of full love, of abundance, of complete brotherhood, of freedom and peace, sharply contradict the political reality of the present kingdom, with its system of suffering and violence, of exploitation, of selfishness, of artificial scarcity, of private ownership of the means of production, of war and repression. . . . This contradiction is political in nature. The irreconcilable contradiction between present and future takes on an imminent character because both kingdoms exist within the same space: within this one history (Silva 1981, 173).

JESUS, ANNOUNCING LIFE, KILLED AS A SUBVERSIVE

Jesus is identified with the poor, and, listening to the poor who ask a new kingdom of him, he acts on behalf of those poor. In doing so, he subverts the established order. Therefore the order kills him.

If Jesus had respected the law, the Jewish "constitution" of the Sanhedrin, the reigning order and the socially acceptable virtues, he would have died an old man within the confines of the city. But he died outside *the city—crucified.*
Enrique Dussel, *Ethics and the Theology of Liberation*

In the four accounts of the life of Jesus in the New Testament, extraordinary importance is given to his death and to the events surrounding it; in fact about one-third of each is dedicated to this part of the story. In our churches the liturgical year maintains this same focus; Jesus' death and its meaning are central to our faith.

And yet much of our reflection on his death stands in sharp contradiction to what the Gospels have to say about it—and we are not even aware of that fact. We speak glibly about what Jesus said and did, and consider ourselves to be his followers without taking into account that he was killed because of what he said and how he lived. Jesus was condemned to death by the religious and political authorities of his day as a criminal, an enemy of the established order.

Jesus was killed for political reasons, yet we have so spiritualized the story of his life that this fact escapes our comprehension. In the days when students at Princeton Seminary occasionally raised their voices in protest, a small group scheduled a demonstration for Maundy Thursday and informed the faculty of their plans. The faculty, after much consideration of the matter, asked the students to postpone the demonstration. The faculty did not consider it appropriate to allow anything having to do with politics to disturb the spiritual mood of Holy Week.

Perhaps it is on this point—the thorough and complacent depoliticization of Jesus by First World Christians—that Latin American Christians can shock us into a reexamination of our faith. As growing numbers of men and women who take Jesus' life and teaching seriously face suffering and death, their witness raises some disturbing questions about the relationship between Jesus and politics in his time and in our own time as well. Why would the "good" people want to kill someone who went about doing good? Why would those whose responsibility it was to preserve a just social order and defend everything that was sacred kill someone struggling to establish God's kingdom of justice?

One thing I think is clear. This happens only in extreme cases when those charged with protecting church and society decide that the death of someone is necessary for others to keep on living. We consider eliminating another human being only when our survival is threatened.

In the world of Jesus, as in ours today, the survival of the established order means the perpetuation of injustice against the poor. Even when it is based on a system of law, supported by electoral processes, and blessed by religious authorities, the existing order is one in which many have to suffer in order for others, often only a few, to enjoy life; many are denied the most basic necessities of life so that others can be affluent; many are kept in inferior positions, humiliated, and denied a sense of worth so that a few may enjoy power and prestige. And we, like those before us, work overtime to justify doing nothing about it. By word and deed Jesus exposed this system of evil and challenged the rationalizations used to sustain it. For this he had to die.

By focusing exclusively on the need of the other—the poor person standing before us—Jesus lays bare the hypocrisy of the religious fundamentalists. They declare that all they are doing is defending the authority of and obeying God. In reality they are using God to justify and preserve their own privileged positions. Declaring that a living God, meeting us in the other in need, demands new responses in a new historical situation, Jesus exposed as idolatrous all attempts to absolutize past responses.

Jesus was not only disrespectful of those in positions of authority while exalting those of low degree, but he also challenged the structures and ideology of domination that keep many persons down and give others power over them. In the Sermon on the Mount he undercut the absolute authority of a sacrosanct order and made room for the human person to emerge fully in the context of personal response to God and to neighbor.

As we have become aware of all this, we have become accustomed to speaking in a general way of the value of the person. But Jesus was quite specific: he affirmed the worth of the worthless; he gave a privileged place and a unique vocation in history to those who have no place. He declared that the kingdom of God belongs to the poor and likened the messianic age to a great banquet to which "the poor and lame and blind and maimed" are welcomed (Luke 14:15–24). And in Matthew 25, Jesus announces that in our encounter with the hungry and naked, the sick and imprisoned, we meet with no one less than himself.

Jesus' decision to speak and act in this way led him to give so much importance to the liberation of others that he could not concern himself about his own liberation. He was treated by those in power as the poor have always been treated: he was hated, denounced, and accused, with no institution to defend him, no power on his side. His dignity, his security, his very life were taken away from him; he died as the poor die. And as the one who announced the approach of the messianic kingdom for the poor, he was forced to face the fact that "his messianism must be interpreted in terms of apparent failure and ruin. . . . He must be content with the tremendous political violence of his truth being sacrificed before the eyes of his enemies" (Ellacuría 1976, 60).

The death of Jesus lays bare the logic of the powerful and the wealthy, the consequences of what they do as seen in the living death of the poor, and the length to which they will go to preserve what they have.

THE BIRTH OF HOPE IN THE MIDST OF DEATH

*If they kill me, I will rise again in the Salvadoran people.
. . . If those Salvadorans who threaten to assassinate me
should go so far as to carry out their threats, I want you to
know that I now offer my blood to God for justice and the
resurrection of El Salvador. . . . If God accepts the sacrifice
of my life, my hope is that my blood will be like a seed of
liberty and a sign that our hopes will soon become a reality.*
                                    Archbishop Oscar Romero

The wealthy and the powerful, the religious and political rulers of the time, had little trouble putting Jesus to death, thus defeating, they believed, his attempt to subvert the established order. The movement that had begun to take shape around him was completely crushed; his few followers, humiliated and scared, were scattered. But according to the four Gospels, his death turned out to be the beginning rather than the end of the story.

They declare that Jesus, after being executed as a political criminal, was very much alive in the midst of his disciples. The handful of poor and marginal men and women who had trusted his word that God's kingdom of justice was about to be established only to see it all come to nothing were suddenly once again filled with joy and with hope. Those who had been scattered came back together, formed a new community in which they shared all that they had, and found themselves strangely empowered to continue what Jesus had started and carry it far beyond the narrow borders of Israel.

Nearly two thousand years later, a conservative archbishop heard the cry of the poor of El Salvador, saw the injustice they were victims of, and spoke out about it. When priests in his diocese who had defended the poor were assassinated along with lay persons who shared their concerns, he understood and denounced the economic and political *system* that was capable of perpetrating such evil. When he declared that the church is called to be the voice of the voiceless, supported the development of base communities of the poorest, and pleaded with the soldiers to disobey orders to kill peasants, he knew his life was in danger. But the significant thing is that Archbishop Romero looked at what was happening around him and to him in the light of the resurrection of Jesus. He used that event to interpret his own history.

On a recent visit to El Salvador, I came in contact with an extraordinary company of men and women who were following this same path. Priests and nuns, university professors, labor leaders, peasants, and women working with human rights organizations: these people interpreted the struggle going on in their country from the perspective of the resurrection and were somehow empowered to face, every day, the possibility of being killed because of their witness.

Across the centuries New Testament scholars have made many

attempts to explain what happened on the first Easter; systematic theologians have written volumes about what it means. Whatever we may make of their efforts, one fact stands out: Between first-century Palestine and El Salvador today, the resurrection of Jesus has, at times, so captivated the thought and life of men and women that it has radically transformed their perception of events occurring around them. It has led them to interpret their history in a way that directly contradicts the major assumptions on which societies and nations are built. When lived out it has often led to death—and new life.

For the poor and apparently powerless, the resurrection is a promise that someday, somehow, justice will be done. Saint Paul gave classic expression to this faith when he said: "God chose what is weak in the world to shame the strong, God chose what is low and despised in the world, even things that are not, to bring to nothing things that are" (1 Cor. 1:27–29). In a refugee camp in San Salvador I met women and men who today live by that hope. I talked with women whose husbands, sons, and daughters had been killed by "men in uniform" and who themselves had been raped and tortured by them. I listened to a few men who were alive only because they had not been at home when their village was destroyed by soldiers. Women told me how members of their families had been massacred because they participated in a basic Christian community, belonged to a cooperative, or attended adult literacy classes. And yet with this history, living precariously, these survivors were learning new trades, organizing production cooperatives, and taking responsibility for the children of their former neighbors. In the midst of their deep sorrow, they were vital, courageous, compassionate, and generous, and they were sustained by hope that their cause would be vindicated.

For those who choose to become involved in the struggle for justice and, often to their surprise, find themselves on a *via crucis*, the resurrection sustains hope that social transformation is possible and enriches their lives. In contact with black friends who were involved in the civil rights movement and with Korean students defending human rights, I have sensed the power of this faith as I have seen them living dangerously and moving in and out of prison with rare confidence and courage.

At the same time, the resurrection stands as a constant witness to those in power that they are fighting a losing battle when they go to any length to preserve what they have. How often in our Western history have we seen that those who crucify the bearers of a messianic vision not only become the agents of death but end up destroying themselves as well? In Vietnam, U.S. confidence in and use of its power led to defeat, ruptured the social fabric of the United States, and devastated the lives of thousands of young soldiers. And if the U.S. government continues to participate in the killing of the poor in Central America, it will reap a whirlwind there as well.

Across the centuries the churches of Christendom have spoken all too glibly about the resurrection. Easter has become a time when we celebrate the victory of life over death. We affirm that when we are defeated we can expect new possibilities to open before us. But if we keep our eyes focused on the resurrection of Jesus of Nazareth, we will be led to a somewhat different conclusion: only as we experience in some way the humiliation, rejection, abandonment, and defeat that come from taking up the cause of the poor and powerless against the principalities and powers of the established order, can we await expectantly the emergence of life out of death. This, I believe, is what Saint Paul meant when he declared that only as we learn to "die daily" to what we have gained and achieved for ourselves can we know what resurrection is all about and experience its reality and power.

THE LIBERATION OF THE POOR
THROUGH THE RENUNCIATION OF POWER

Jesus Christ, . . . though he was rich, yet for your sake he became poor, so that by his poverty you might become rich.
2 Cor. 8:9

Our recovery of the social and political dimensions of Jesus' messiahship leaves us with a gnawing question: If we believe that Jesus of Nazareth initiated a new era of liberation of oppressed peoples, how is it that their situation has changed so little in the last two thousand years?

I was recently confronted by this question while teaching a class on liberation theology. Most of the students were pastors from Third World countries or from black and Hispanic neighborhoods in the New York area. Several were women deeply concerned about the oppression of their sex. As they read the writings of Latin American theologians and reread their Bibles, they saw, more clearly than they had before, that the prophets were primarily concerned about justice to the poor. Some of them perceived, for the first time in their lives, that Jesus identified himself with those who were most marginal, declared that the kingdom of God belonged to them, and was killed for political reasons. But as this new awareness grew and they became more sensitive to the suffering around them, they found it impossible to answer the question: Why the long delay in the liberation promised by Jesus?

One pastor of a large ghetto church declared: "If I preached this message, many in my congregation would become completely disillusioned and leave the church; they know that the coming of Jesus hasn't changed their situation." A woman student said: "If Jesus is the liberator of women, why has it taken him two thousand years to get around to it?" Those who were more conservative theologically insisted that, whatever the social implications of Jesus' message, his concern was primarily spiritual. Others concluded that he had been mistaken. He had counted on God's intervention to establish the new order of justice and equality, and that simply had not happened.

Rereading the Gospels with these reactions in mind, it became clear to me that the apparent powerlessness of Jesus the Messiah in history was very much in line with what he said and did during his lifetime. In fact Jesus seems to have gone out of his way not only to renounce the use of power as domination over other people but also to cut away all supports for it in the religious realm.

Whenever his disciples spoke of him as the Messiah, he lost no time in declaring that this meant becoming a servant and following the path of suffering and defeat. He categorically refused to become an agent of oppressive power. In his daily dealing with those who gathered around him, most of them outcasts from society, he showed such a remarkable capacity to affirm their worth and raise them up that they were not cowed by his mysterious power to heal and feed them. At the well in Samaria, Jesus entered into dialogue with someone who the good Jews of his time would have rejected outright: a woman, belonging to a despised minority group, known as a sinner. Yet he so affirmed her as a person that she ended up discovering her own truth and speaking in her own voice. He spoke of God as Father rather than using images suggesting mystery and power, and he died abandoned by God who intervenes in human affairs.

As men and women in Latin America have followed the example of Jesus in relating to the poor, they have arrived at a new understanding of what Jesus intended in his renunciation of power. They have come to realize how religious and political power has been used to humiliate and dehumanize the poor, to convince them that they have no worth and can do nothing. And with this they have perceived that the poor can move toward abundant life only as they discover their own worth, learn to speak in their own voice, and take charge of their lives. The Latin Americans call this becoming *subjects* of their life and destiny. Perhaps for Jesus the messianic era could become a reality for the downtrodden only as conditions were created for their emergence in history as subjects. This is what he set out to do.

In his relationships with his humble followers, he created conditions for them to emerge in this way; with his words and his actions he undercut the authority not only of those in power in religious and political circles but of the myths that sustained them. He urged the poor gathered around him to approach God the Father boldly and demand what they needed: "Ask, and it will be given you; seek, and you will find; knock, and it will be opened to you" (Luke 11:9). And he further indicated that his own physical absence was necessary to open more space for them so that, guided by the Holy Spirit or "Spirit of the Father," they would discover the truth, do even greater works than he had done (John 14:12), and speak out courageously in the presence of the governors and kings before whom they would be dragged (Matt. 10:16–20).

For Jesus the oppressed could only be liberated if they were the agents of their own liberation. The Messiah would not rob them of their responsibility for creating history and working out their own destiny, even if this required a long historical struggle.

I find it especially significant that this emphasis on the poor as subjects is at the heart of the first social revolution in modern times in which Christians have played a decisive role. In Nicaragua I realized that the base communities established by the Catholic church among the peasants and in the poorest barrios of the cities had made it possible for the poor to be in the forefront of that struggle for liberation. I was amazed by the perception they have of their new place and responsibility in that nation and by the tremendous energy this has released for social reconstruction. In fact the revolutionary government has acknowledged this new status of the poor by taking steps to encourage popular movements and to institutionalize this exercise of power from below.

It is still too early to predict the eventual outcome of the Nicaraguan Revolution. But if we look at it from the perspective of the revolutionary process initiated by the prophets and by Jesus of Nazareth, we may be justified in drawing one conclusion: in the Nicaraguan Revolution the liberation and empowerment of the lowly has been carried one step further. What was once only a dream has become a real possibility within history. This fact will inspire other, perhaps stronger, movements of liberation among the poor elsewhere in Central and South America and in the Caribbean.

Chapter 4

When Empires Decline

The preaching of the Cross is, I know, nonsense to those who are involved in this dying world, but to us who are being saved from that death it is nothing less than the power of God.

You don't see among you many of the wise (according to this world's judgment) nor many of the ruling class, nor many from the noblest families. But God has chosen what the world calls foolish to shame the wise; he has chosen what the world calls weak to shame the strong. He has chosen things of little strength and small repute, yes and even things which have no real existence to explode the pretensions of the things that are.

1 Cor. 1:18, 26–28; J. B. Phillips translation

THEOLOGY AND THE CRISIS OF THE ROMAN EMPIRE

The followers of Jesus who laid the foundation for the emergence of the church were largely from the lower classes. According to the Book of Acts, the first congregation sprang up in Jerusalem as the result of an overwhelming spiritual experience associated with the outpouring of the Holy Spirit. For those caught up in it, faith in Jesus Christ led to the practice of a primitive form of communism: "There was not a needy person among them, for as many as were possessors of lands or houses sold them, and brought the proceeds of what was sold and laid it at the apostles' feet; and distribution was made to each as any had need'' (Acts 4:34-35). As the church spread across the Roman Empire, it attracted primarily the humble and the disinherited. The early Christians were *outsiders*. They had no place within the structures of power of their society, and most of them had no recognized place within the dominant culture. Their alienation was intensified by the fact that they were considered to be subversives and were periodically persecuted during the first three hundred years of the church's existence.

During that time the Christians lived out and articulated a vibrant faith that would eventually provide the foundation for a new culture and a new society. They kept alive and were sustained by Jesus' expectation of the imminent establishment of the kingdom of God. They also came to believe that in the life, death, and resurrection of Jesus of Nazareth, God's self had been revealed and had intervened in human history. Their God was the God of Israel, who was known as the creator of the universe and the lord of history and whose purpose for human life had been revealed in the liberation of an enslaved people and in Jesus' inauguration of a new order of justice and peace in the world. Consequently, as Christian thinkers strove to understand their faith, they saw everything that was happening in human life and in the world as part of *one great drama of redemption*. Humankind, created in a state of perfection, had departed from that state and fallen into sin. But the redeemer had come and was at work healing the wounds inflicted by men and women on themselves: "God was in Christ reconciling the world to himself" (2 Cor. 5:19). Human life had a goal and those who shared it found their lives filled with meaning and purpose.

Because the early Christian theologians made use of Greek categories of thought that were quite inadequate for dealing with the concrete realities of historical existence and its transformation, when we read what they wrote we often tend to think of redemption as the struggle of individual souls for salvation in a future life. *What we fail to see is that these theological developments offered a way out of the dead end in which life and classical culture were caught at the time of the decline and fall of the Roman Empire. This vision of and hope for a world redeemed came from the underclass in the empire. Their faith enabled them to respond*

*to the crisis of their time when the wise and powerful within the
dominant political and cultural system could not.*

For an understanding of how this happened, many of us are
greatly indebted to Charles Norris Cochrane. In his book *Christianity and Classical Culture* he traces the decline of the Roman
Empire and of the cultural system on which it was based. At the
same time he portrays the gradual development of a type of Christian thought that exposed the crisis of the empire, challenged the
basic assumptions of classical culture, offered a new starting
point for thought, and laid the foundation for a new era in Western history.

Cochrane begins his story with the establishment of the *Pax
Augusta* in the first century A.D. The Emperor Augustus had initiated a new era of imperial glory, believed by many to represent the
final form of organized society. Peace reigned not only in the
center of the empire but also on its far-flung borders. The
economy was functioning well. A political system based on confidence in the "virtue and fortune" of the emperor seemed to offer
a permanent solution to the problems of the body politic. The rule
of law was firmly established; human impulses and passions appeared to be under control. Those in a privileged position within
that society could look forward to a good life of stability, prosperity, and leisure.

This dream did not last for long. By the third century disillu-
sionment had set in. A process of social disintegration had begun.
The rule of law had given way to political anarchy. Economic and
social distress were evident everywhere. As the internal problems
of the empire became more acute, conquered barbarian peoples
on the fringes tried to break free. The effort to hold the empire
together thus demanded more and more attention from the rulers
and ever greater military expenditures. In a situation calling for
dynamic action, the empire was immobilized.

In the fourth century Constantine, in a desperate attempt to
inject new life in a moribund body, embraced Christianity as the
state religion. He tried to reestablish a peaceful order, as it had
existed earlier. He pressed for moral and social reforms, the reconstruction of the family, and the provision of charity for some
of those in need. He was convinced that these efforts together
with the new energies provided by the Christian religion would

save the system. It didn't work. The new religion did not check the process of social decay, and the "social and economic forces which were grinding the life out of the provincials continued to operate remorselessly" (Cochrane 1940, 217).

Toward the end of the fourth century, Theodosius made one last attempt to save the empire by combining despotism and the use of Christianity as *the* religion of the state. He suppressed paganism and fought against Christian heresies, counting on orthodoxy to provide the principle of social integration. His hope was to "achieve a new world without sacrificing any essential elements of the old" (p. 338). But this attempt to use God for the maintenance of human institutions also failed. After Theodosius the empire staggered toward its end.

In his analysis of the disintegration of the empire, Cochrane contends that it was doomed not because its problems were insoluble but because classical thought was incapable of responding to the crisis. He speaks of a "moral and intellectual failure, a failure of the Graeco-Roman mind" (p. 157). As society fell apart, men and women had no way of understanding what was happening around them and were gripped by a haunting fear of the unknown. Explaining disaster in terms of bad luck or fate proved highly inadequate. And greater emphasis on the divinity of the emperor, trusting in his power to order society, eventually seemed quite absurd as the distance between reality and myth widened.

Classical culture could not find meaning in change. It thus failed to do justice to growth and development in the individual and in society. Its vision of the future was based on an idealized past. Consequently, social salvation could only be found in conformity to established models and structures, and those most threatened fought most desperately to preserve them. This effort was destined to fail. History does not repeat itself; situations call for new responses. As Cochrane remarks, classical culture ended up transforming the traditional order into a principle of control, which meant extending "to the dead a prescriptive right to govern the living" (p. 104).

The situation called for the release of tremendous energies in ventures of social creativity. But this could not happen without a compelling vision of a new order. Without it those in positions of power and privilege had no higher goal than to use the system for their greatest private advantage. Those who might have taken the initiative in finding new solutions to social, economic, and political problems had neither the will nor the energies necessary to do so. The impulses which had propelled Rome to the height of its greatness were languishing.

As this process of decay gradually advanced in culture and society, something radically different was happening within the Christian community scattered across the empire. Theologians were looked down upon by the cultural elite. They had no place in sophisticated circles of philosophers. But having no stake within the dominant culture, they were able to perceive the defects of its rationale, the limitations it imposed on human experience, and the bankruptcy of its system of values. They were free to create a counterculture, and that is what they did. For these theologians the life, the teachings, and the crucifixion of a Palestinian Jew (all three considered to be "foolishness" by the Greeks) provided richer insights into human nature and destiny than all the great works of the Greek philosophers, and they proceeded boldly to spell this out. Moreover they were convinced that faith in this Jesus was the source of new life in a dying world, and they witnessed to its power.

Athanasius, bishop of Alexandria for forty-five years, was the leading architect of this theological counterculture during the fourth century. Living far from the center of the empire, he was nevertheless exiled five times by the Roman emperors because of the boldness of his stand. His essay *On the Incarnation of the Word* is an excellent illustration of how these early Christian thinkers went about developing a new paradigm for thought and life.

The bishop begins his treatise admitting the "seeming low estate of the Word," which the "Greeks laugh to scorn," and then proceeds to develop an alternative conceptual framework from which to interpret what is happening in human life and the world. He has sufficient confidence in his own intellectual system to challenge the thought of both Jews and Greeks. But his primary emphasis is upon the dramatic transformation of human life which occurs wherever the Christian message is preached. This new reality, not the crisis of empire, is the center of his attention;

it is a sign of the future reign of peace prophesied by Isaiah, which Jesus Christ "was to usher in." And the power of this faith is confirmed by the willingness of so many young men and women to die for it. Less than one hundred years later, Augustine was able to give a definitive and systematic formulation to this new perspective. By that time the crisis of the dominant culture had reached the point where he could declare that, of the once famous Stoics and Epicureans, "only their ashes survive."

For those whose well-being depended upon the survival of the empire, the Fall of Rome could only mean the loss of everything they valued, the end of civilization, and the unleashing of anarchy upon the world. Christians, who had lived as pilgrims and foreigners in imperial society for so long, had a different perception of what was happening. Their fate was not tied to that of the empire; moreover the future they envisaged was that of "the world to come." Thus they were able to see the defects of the established order as well as the injustices it perpetrated and view the process of social and political disintegration with detachment. In Cochrane's words: Christianity regarded the Roman order "as doomed to extinction by reason of its inherent deficiencies, and it confidently anticipated the period of its dissolution as a prelude to the establishment of the earthly sovereignty of Christ" (p. 177).

This unusual stance was sustained by a formidable intellectual effort that brought about a revolution in thought. A group of theologians, considered ignoramuses by those instructed in the wisdom of the Greeks, based their reflection on a religious heritage focusing on two strange historical events: the liberation of an enslaved people in Egypt and the teaching of a Galilean Jew who announced the coming of a messianic kingdom and was killed as a subversive for doing so. The result of their efforts was the articulation of a perspective on life and the world that created conditions for a new experiment in living at a time when the fountain of life of classical culture had dried up. That perspective inspired a struggle to create a new social order in the midst of the ruins left by a dying empire.

For most of us today the thought of these early theologians does not seem at all revolutionary; it may not even make sense to us. This is due in part to the fact that it is so much a part of our history that we take it for granted. Moreover, their categories of thought are no longer part of our daily discourse. In the fourth century, however, what they accomplished represented an important breakthrough in a number of areas of intellectual consideration: the relationship between God and history and nature, between the divine and human, and between love and power.

The faith of Israel was, first of all, faith in a God who was active in history and had liberated a people. As it developed further, this action in history was universalized, and this God was also recognized as the creator of the universe, active in the world of nature. As Christian theologians dealt with the problems of their time from the perspective of this faith, they were able to challenge the belief that nature and history were independent realms subject to natural necessity, realms alien to both God and humankind. They affirmed that the universe was the product of the free creative activity of God and that all nature and history were subordinate to this God and related directly to the divine purpose. One consequence of this was that the fundamental split in the Greek world between God as being and the process of becoming was overcome, opening the way both for a new integrated worldview and for a new interpretation of human experience.

From the first, Christians were convinced that there was something divine about Jesus of Nazareth, that he was the *revelation* of God. The God who was active in the world and in history had appeared in the midst of history in the life, death, and resurrection of Jesus. As a result men and women who believed in and responded to Jesus Christ would be enabled to understand what was going on around them. They would be able to perceive the presence and the work of the Redeemer in all spheres of life and history. In the language of the theologians, Jesus was the Logos, the Truth, *"credo ut intelligam."* Faith opens the way for us to understand. And Jesus, the Redeemer, is the revelation of the beneficent activity of God in the world; the Christian is not engaged in a futile attempt to read values into nature and history or impose them on nature and history. The Christian is engaged in the task of apprehending those values and potentialities present there but often not perceived.

At the heart of Christian faith was the belief that Jesus Christ was at one and the same time fully divine and fully human. The theological debates of the fourth century had to do with the problem of how to express and develop conceptually what that meant. Without going into the intricacies of their arguments, we can understand what they were struggling to affirm and the importance of it: God has a human face. In Jesus of Nazareth, God assumes full humanity. The creator of the universe and the lord of history is fundamentally concerned about the redemption of humankind. At the same time Jesus, as a human being, makes visible in history what human beings are capable of. We are therefore called to look at human life from the perspective of what it can become. In the language of that time, God became human so that human beings might become like God.

Most of us today do not get excited about the doctrine of the Trinity, with its complicated formulations attempting to find and describe precisely the right relationships among God the Creator, Jesus Christ the Redeemer, and the Holy Spirit as the principle of movement and energy. But all of us have been profoundly affected by what these theologians accomplished through their debates: they came to perceive and speak of the order of nature and history as the realms in which the spirit of life is at work, the milieu in which human life can move toward fulfillment. They were able to bring about a union of body and spirit and thus conceive of human nature being realized through the redemption of the flesh. As a consequence of their worldview, history was perceived as the realm of freedom for human beings, and human life and history could be thought of in terms of growth and development.

The crisis of classical culture provided an opportunity for those who were marginal to it and scorned by it to provide a new understanding of nature and history, a new order of truth and value, and a new project for human fulfillment.

This trinitarian theology made an enormous difference in the political realm. Christians came to realize that their fate was not bound up with the fate of the empire. For them the possibility of finding meaning in life and in history did not depend upon its survival. If Jesus Christ was the only Son of God the Father, there was no place for other divine beings. The emperor was not a god. But if the emperor was not a divine being, then there was nothing ultimate or sacred about the structures and values of the empire.

The struggle of the theologians to establish God as the creator and source of movement in nature and history led to the desacralization of those realms and thus undercut the power of chance and fate as interpretative principles. In their stead, they offered another possibility of making sense out of what was happening in the world. Ambrose declared that time, space, and matter are "not gods but gifts." Augustine asserted that "the stars are not the fate of Christ, but Christ is the fate of the stars." Empires rise and fall, not by fate or chance, but in the providence of God.

Moreover, if God's action in nature and history aims at the redemption of humanity, then *history is moving toward that goal in and through the decline and fall of empires.* Christians must then be concerned to discern how this redemptive process is going and look at what is happening in the political order from that perspective. For Augustine this meant that the basic struggle in history is between "the love of power and the power of love." The empire functions according to the former principle. Its leaders claim that they are defending freedom and security. What they are really doing is trying to justify their greed for human glory and for material prosperity. Their lust for possessions drives them to impose the yoke of servitude on other peoples; their fear of losing what they have is the foundation for their self-deception. The church, on the other hand, is the divine society, that community which orients its life by the power of love and seeks to make that principle operative in the world. Oriented toward this goal, Christians can find meaning in an otherwise irrational world and live and act responsibly even as the darkness gathers around them.

Ultimately these theologians offered a way out of the pessimism and desperation of their time because they looked expectantly toward the future. They believed in the possibility of a new order beyond the collapse of the status quo. Cochrane speaks of Augustine's "millennial vision" which held out to human beings the prospect of the fulfillment of their humanity. It was a vision of a "divine society," of a kingdom of goodness and, more than this, a kingdom "already present among men, if only they have the wit and the desire to see it." Cochrane ends his study of the relationship between Christianity and classical culture on this note. For Augustine, he says, "history is prophecy; i.e., its true significance lies not in the past, nor in the present, but in the future, the life of 'the world to come' " (p. 516).

THEOLOGY AND THE CRISIS OF EMPIRE TODAY

During the latter half of the twentieth century, we have witnessed the decline and partial collapse of the empires over which the industrial nations of the West have ruled. In the United States most of us have not thought of our country as an imperial power. And yet, Henry Luce articulated the dream of many at the end of World War II when he spoke of "The American Century." Since that time, as our economic, political, and military power has developed more and more, we have tended to use it imperialistically to serve our own ends.

But as our exercise of power has grown, our world has become more insecure. Economic crises, U.S. military involvement in Vietnam, Central America, the Middle East, and the Caribbean, and the threat of nuclear war have aroused deep anxiety in the souls of many in the First World and have led to protest movements calling into question the present order as well as the values on which it is based. At the same time, Third World countries that see themselves as victims of First World power and exploitation are challenging the Western industrial nations' dominant role in their parts of the world. Uncertain any longer of the future, we in the First World are gripped by fear of the unknown. In our fear we glorify our past and try to impose it on a situation calling for bold new solutions. Bound by the limits of our ideology, we are incapable of imagining alternatives to a system which is no longer working.

How desperately we need today a religious faith capable of doing for our time what Christianity did during the decline of the Roman Empire! The classical theological formulations worked out at that time responded creatively to that particular historical context. And if those formulations are still central to our faith, should we not assume that they can make a similar contribution today? That could happen—but only if we are able to find solutions to a couple of major problems, both of which the Latin American theologians can help us overcome. The first of these is that the worldview, the concepts, and the language of the fourth century are not ours today. Consequently, the perspective on life and history developed then can mean something to us only as it is expressed in a new language capable of interpreting our world.

The present moment calls for re-creation, not repetition.

Also, the theology that became a subversive force in the Roman Empire has played a major role in creating and sustaining the empires now in decline. And the church, which was originally shaped by its marginal existence as a persecuted minority for three hundred years, has been on the side of those in power for most of the last fifteen hundred years. A theology once capable of bringing about a "revolution in thought and action" may be able to do so once again but only if its comfortable accommodation with the established order is sharply challenged.

This is what the Latin American theologians are doing. Most of them have been trained in Western Europe and take this classical theology as the foundation for their thought. They take for granted the relationship between God and the realms of nature and history as defined by the doctrine of the Trinity. They look at the historical process from the perspective of redemption and interpret what that means in the light of the life, death, and resurrection of Jesus Christ.

But their theological work is being done outside the great centers of imperial power. They share the interest of many of their generation in the richness and vitality of their indigenous cultures. And they have been compelled by their faith to identify with the struggle of the dispossessed in their societies. As a result, *they speak of the great drama of redemption as the struggle for liberation on the part of the oppressed.* God's action in history focuses on the struggle of the poor to create a new social order. Classical theological language is, once again, a subversive force. Here I want to give three examples of what this means.

1. The major theological battles of the fourth century led to the affirmation of something profoundly scandalous for the Greek mind: the *incarnation* of God in humanity. This doctrine brought together realms until that time completely separated from each other: God and human persons, the eternal and the temporal, being and becoming, spirit and body. Today Latin American theologians are saying something no less scandalous for our world: *The incarnation means that God became a poor human being.* For two thousand years the gospel stories have stated this very clearly, but most Christian thinkers have given no theological significance to it. Saint Paul did when he declared that Jesus

Christ "did not count equality with God a thing to be grasped, but emptied himself, taking the form of a slave" (Phil. 2:6–7).

For the Latin Americans the implications of this are inescapable. In the words of Alejandro Cussiánovich,

> Christ enters humanity historically through the mediation of the poor. He is a poor person, not just a member of humanity in some vague, undefined sense. . . . The historical humanity which he takes on himself is the humanity of the poor—the human, or rather, inhuman conditions in which the marginalized classes and the oppressed common people live their lives [Cussiánovich 1979, 113].

If we take this seriously, we will no longer be content to say that God became human so that human beings can become divine. Rather we must affirm that God became a poor person so that those most dehumanized by exploitation and oppression can have a full human life. This is the goal of the divine intervention in history.

If we believe that God's assumption of our humanity means identification with the suffering, the weakness, the death-in-life of the poor, then "the liberating love of God is ever linked historically to the poor" (Cussiánovich 1979, 85). Their struggle provides the clue to the essence of God's redemptive work in history. Those who once believed that their misery was decreed by fate or the will of God now see that God is struggling for and with them; those who were nobodies with no place have a unique calling. Likewise, if Jesus as God incarnate stands with the poor and looks at what is happening in the world from that perspective, then those who would be his disciples have no choice but to do the same. As one Latin American writer remarks: In the Book of Hebrews, the author says that Christ, the pioneer of our salvation through suffering, is not ashamed to call us his brothers. The bigger question today may be whether *we* are ashamed to call *this* Christ *our* brother.

Virgilio Elizondo, director of the Mexican-American Cultural Center in San Antonio, Texas, gives us a clear indication of what this reinterpretation of the incarnation can mean for a marginalized people in our midst. In *Galilean Journey* he declares that "the human scandal of God's way does not begin with the cross but with the historico-cultural incarnation of his Son in Galilee" (Elizondo 1983, 53). Galileans were considered sociologically inferior by their own people and culturally inferior by the great powers of the world. They were "materially, psychologically, sociologically, and culturally poor." In other words they were rejects, and "Jesus entered and left human society as a reject" (p. 55).

Elizondo then develops what he calls the "Galilean principle": "what human beings reject, God chooses as his very own" (p. 91). In this light the Mexican-American experience of rejection and marginalization is no longer a human curse; it is rather a position of privilege from which Mexican-Americans can make a unique contribution toward the creation of a new society. Those who have been made to feel inferior can appreciate what it means to be affirmed as full human beings, and this new self-image releases new power. Those who have been wounded can become the healers of the illness of the existing society. Living in two different worlds they can affirm the values of each and work for and contribute to the type of social interaction that will enrich all of us.

2. The world, across the centuries, has known many religions of salvation. What is distinctive about Christianity is its belief that we are saved through the death and resurrection of a human being, Jesus of Nazareth, a man of flesh and blood. The liberation theologians take all this for granted but insist that we must speak much more concretely about it: we are saved by the death and resurrection of a poor man, who shared the lot of the poor and was killed because he took up their cause against the wealthy and powerful.

Therefore we cannot speak about sin and salvation in Christian terms apart from this concrete social reality. The sin from which Christ saves us has a social dimension; it is related directly to the use of power to exploit and destroy the weak and powerless. When we declare that Christ died for our sins, we are not speaking of some sort of expiation in order to satisfy an angry God. Christ died for our sins because he so upset the established order that he had to be killed by those who had a stake in it. The resurrection of Jesus represents much more than the general triumph of life over death. Saint Paul speaks of the reign of death, an order of domination on the part of "principalities and powers" that is moving toward death and destroys those who are its victims. The resurrection means that the power of this order has been broken and a new movement toward life has begun for those deprived of it. If we dare to say that we have risen with Christ, we are declaring that we are being set free from our bondage to this order of exploitation and destruction and are discovering a new life as we engage in the struggle for liberation.

Various New Testament writers claim that the salvation wrought through the death and resurrection of Jesus of Nazareth has a cosmic dimension to it. For Saint Paul this meant not only the redemption of the whole realm of creation which had been groaning in travail but also the transformation of history. Christ is the end of history, the goal toward which it moves. With his resurrection, this end time has already begun. The theologians of the fourth and fifth centuries, as we have seen, developed all this much further. For them Jesus Christ, the Logos, was seen as the principle of order and movement in nature and history.

Here too the Latin American theologians, while taking this perspective for granted, insist on greater concreteness. If God redeems the world through a poor person and if the central event in this salvation history is the crucifixion of Jesus because of his identification with the poor in their struggle, then *the poor and their struggle must be at the very center of our interpretation of what is happening in nature and history.* As Cussiánovich puts it:

> The poor are the centerpiece in salvation history, the necessary mediating link in the relationship between God and human beings, between human beings themselves, and between human beings and nature. The universe can no longer be the stage for relations of injustice, inequality, and discrimination. It must become the new earth, the setting for relations of authentic kinship [p. 114].

Although insisting on the uniqueness of what happened in the life, death, and resurrection of Jesus of Nazareth, Christians have always claimed that the redemptive process initiated by Jesus Christ continues in history. Jesus himself continues to be present and active in the world. This has been expressed by a number of metaphors: Christ is seen as the head of the body, the church. The church is spoken of as the continuation of the incarnation. In some circles emphasis is placed on the presence of and the power of the Holy Spirit.

Here again the theologians of liberation insist on much greater specificity. For them the central fact of the historical process is that the great majority of men and women in the world continue to be crucified by a social order in which the few benefit at their expense. Therefore any attempt to speak of the continued presence of Christ in history must take this into account.

Ignacio Ellacuría has spelled out the implications of this in a compelling essay entitled "El pueblo crucificado." His thesis is that salvation comes through the crucifixion of Christ *and of the oppressed.* Jesus continues to be crucified in the world through the poor. By bringing together in this way the crucifixion of Jesus and the crucifixion of the poor, the theologians of liberation help to make it possible for the poor to keep hope alive in the midst of their suffering. They can see their struggle in the light of the resurrection of Jesus and thus hope against hope that the kingdom of justice will eventually triumph. Furthermore the crucifixion of Jesus is tied securely to history and, more specifically, to the ongoing suffering of the dispossessed within structures of domination and exploitation. Any attempt to appropriate the cross of Christ to sustain individual piety detached from these social struggles can be seen only as a radical distortion of the Christian message.

3. Theologians have always been concerned about the relationship of faith and history. This concern has increased as Christians have become more aware of the fact that their faith is directly tied to certain historical events and as human attention has turned more and more to what happens to us, individually and collectively, in history. However, much Christian thought has been limited by one assumption: that as Christians we must think in terms of two histories, the history of God's action in the world for our salvation and profane or secular history.

The theologians of liberation challenge this assumption. They consider that it represents the imposition on the Bible of a worldview foreign to it. For instance Gustavo Gutiérrez has made these statements about history: "There is only one history"; "The history of salvation is the very heart of human history!"; and "The historical destiny of humanity must be placed definitively in the salvific horizon" (Gutiérrez 1973, 153). In other words when Christians tell the story of God's great acts for the salvation of the world, they are describing what is happening in history. The historical process is moving toward an end: the full redemption of human life and, more specifically, the full liberation of all those who are poor and oppressed. History is then the process by which the lowly of the world, trampled and exploited by those in power, move toward a full human life as they become the subjects of their own life and destiny.

Those who adopt this perspective perceive movement and purpose in history. Those who have been marginal move to the center of the stage and have reason to hope that their struggle will not always end in defeat and death. And with this all the richness of biblical imagery (for instance, the exodus, Babylonian captivity, crucifixion, and apocalypse) can be drawn on to interpret this struggle for justice. At a time when liberal thought seems incapable of transcending the limits of the established order and Marxism often is locked into an ideological straitjacket, the theology of liberation enriches the language of politics and expands the utopian horizon especially among the masses.

For many today any attempt to perceive meaning and purpose in history borders on the absurd. For the theologians of liberation, however, this perception is an inescapable consequence of their faith in Jesus Christ as he has been understood across the centuries. By dividing history into two periods—B.C. and A.D.— Christians affirmed that with Jesus of Nazareth a new period in history had begun. What the Latin Americans are doing is not only reaffirming this but also spelling it out much more concretely. Jesus initiated a new process of human liberation because of what he said and did. He undercut the authority of all institutions and structures of power in order to make room for the primacy of the human person: "The sabbath was made for man, not man for the sabbath" (Mark 2:27). By declaring that the kingdom of God belongs to the poor, he elevated them to a new position in the world and gave them a special vocation in history. His declaration that God's kingdom of peace and justice was already breaking into history and his emphasis on the imminence of the end of the established order challenged men and women to look at every status quo in the light of a promised future. And he offered those on top a way out by assuring them that in dying to what they have, they will find new life.

Thus by word and deed Jesus launched a new historical era. He set loose in history a force destined to transform it radically. The Christian is free to see and trace this influence of Jesus across the centuries. Severino Croatto describes how this influence made itself felt early within the Roman Empire:

> As a leader, Jesus generates a new symbolical order that culminates in the political sphere. Insofar as the poor are conscienticized, they become a new force. They will be the basis of the primitive church and a decisive factor in the weakening of the Roman Empire. Equality among all people will produce a rupture within the socioeconomic system of the ancient world: the slaves of the Empire will be the revolutionary ferment of the first centuries of the Christian faith. The cult of the emperor-god crumbles at the roots and is demythologized on all levels, thus losing the oppressive function sustained by the mythical ideology [Croatto 1981, 64].

Croatto then goes on to say that all this is only a small indication of the capacity "of the deeds and the words of Jesus to liberate *human beings* from every alienating and oppressive system, whether religious or political" (p. 64).

This same claim has been made by a number of other writers. What they have not yet done is to trace this revolutionary influence of Jesus across the centuries and point to any pattern or logic in it. This, I believe, is an area in which serious historical studies might be of great value. For as I read the history of the West in the light of Jesus of Nazareth, two things stand out. First, the history of the West is the history of revolutions, each of which overcame a process of sclerosis and death and initiated a new era by creating new forms of social organization and a new type of human being. And second, this process of liberation moves "downward." In its earlier stages bishops challenged emperors; lords and citizens stood up against kings. But the process continued until the proletariat challenged those who ruled in the economic sphere, and now, in Latin America and elsewhere, the poorest and most oppressed are demanding that the economic order meet their needs and that they have an opportunity to participate fully in the exercise of public power. To the extent that social movements are faithful to this vision, they may also focus our attention on the direction in which history, under the influence of Jesus, is moving in our time.

Chapter 5

Looking at the World from Below

If the biblical story is essentially that of God's action in history
for the liberation of the enslaved and oppressed persons of the
world, and if Jesus Christ took upon himself the life and struggle
of the poor in order to raise them up to a full human life, then the
most urgent questions we who call ourselves Christians have to
face are these: Where do *we* stand in relation to the poor? What is
our response to their cry?

That response has many facets. One of them has to do with the
perspective from which we perceive what is going on in the world.
Do we look at it *from above* or *from below?* Moses, the prophets,
Jesus, and the leaders of the early church belonged to the lower
classes, the marginal people of their time. They looked at life and
history from where they stood. Jesus so identified himself with
the poor and interpreted life and history from that perspective in
such a radical way that he was quickly eliminated by the religious
and political rulers. If we want to understand and honor his words
and work and faithfully interpret biblical truth, we must do something more than repeat and defend biblical texts. Truth is as much
a matter of perspective as it is of logic. We speak truthfully about
Jesus only when we look at the world from his perspective—from
below.

More than a hundred years ago Karl Marx pointed out that our
social and economic position decisively influences our understanding of society, but we have largely ignored him. In 1942 Dietrich Bonhoeffer, out of his prison experience, wrote these
amazing words:

> There remains an experience of incomparable value. We
> have for once learnt to see the great events of world history
> from below, from the perspective of the outcast, the sus-
> pects, the maltreated, the powerless, the oppressed, the
> reviled—in short, from the perspective of those who suffer
> [Bonhoeffer 1978, 17].

If we take Bonhoeffer's words as prophecy rather than as a
statement of fact, we can say that today in Latin America this
prophecy is being fulfilled. As increasing numbers of men and
women allow their reading of the Gospel and their experience of
faith to shape their perception, some remarkable changes have
occurred. Over the last several years I have tried to listen to what
they are saying and reflect on it in the light of my own experience
in the South Bronx and in North Philadelphia. Out of this have
come several theses about the view from below.

1. By and large those who are underneath see more clearly what
is happening in society than those on top. We need them as our
teachers if we hope to understand the world in which we live.

Time and again I have been forced to recognize this fact. When
I first went to Latin America, I soon realized that those who were
victims of our foreign policy understood how it worked much
better than those who made and administered it. When I tried to
understand racism in the United States, it became clear to me that
the victims had to teach me what it really is. At a conference on
housing in the South Bronx, I sensed that those being pushed out
of their homes had a deeper level of understanding of the problem
than the scholars who had spent years studying it. And on a recent
visit to El Salvador, I was astonished to find that political leaders
with whom I spoke denied the existence of major human rights
violations for which I had massive documentation. Then I realized that in the First World we simply have more subtle ways than
those used in countries like El Salvador to keep the poor, the dis-
abled, and the imprisoned out of our sight and out of our minds.

Only as I associate with the poor can I understand what they
know in their bones, that the society that favors me works against
them. Only while living in the South Bronx did I realize that the
supermarket chains sell inferior products at higher prices there
than in the suburbs. The same school system that prepared my

children to move upward in society often convinces the children of the poor that they cannot get ahead. Government funds for highways, streets, parks, and other services are used more readily in wealthier neighborhoods than in the poor areas where they are most needed. The poor find themselves often harassed by the police to whom we look for help, humiliated in government offices that serve us, and kept waiting for long hours in emergency rooms of hospitals to which we turn expecting immediate attention.

I have learned much more from the poor about the way our society functions as a total system than in the college classroom or in dialogue with well-educated, middle-class persons. Even when we are victims of injustice or become disturbed about what our government is doing in Central America, we rarely concern ourselves about how one social issue is related to others or try to figure out how our society functions *as a system*. The poor, on the other hand, often surprise me by the depth of their understanding of the system they run up against every day. The poor are probably as much affected by the distortion of reality presented through the mass media as I am. But my contact with the dispossessed does more than anything else to show me how I am being brainwashed and forces me to take into account dimensions of reality that do not fit into the stereotypes presented to me daily.

When Jesus announced that the kingdom of God belongs to the poor, he was calling our attention to the fact that they reveal to us what is happening around us. They help to remove the veil under which reality is hidden. If we want to cultivate a Christian perception of the gospel and the world, we need to live in close contact with them and be exposed to their insights and perceptions.

2. To the extent that we look at the world from below, we create space for the poor and outcasts to affirm themselves within their own culture and speak with their own voice. This not only gives them a chance to be human but contributes to the enrichment of us all.

The wealthy and powerful assume that they are superior and look down paternalistically upon those who cannot make it in their world. They take for granted that their way of thinking, their system of values, their culture, and their institutions should be normative. By making them so, they ensure their continued domination. For as long as those on top can impose their way of thinking and acting on those to whom it is alien, the poor will fail to measure up. When this happens, they can be kept out of the mainstream and made to believe that they really are inferior beings.

Amerindians from villages in the high Andes can only feel humiliated when forced to function in a city in which the dominant language, culture, and way of working are totally alien to them. Blacks will score lower than whites on intelligence tests that reflect the experience and thought patterns of middle-class whites. And women in academic institutions are at a disadvantage when expected to use the conceptual categories and abstract linear thought patterns of males.

However, when the oppressed are allowed to find their own way and speak with their own voice, the picture changes dramatically. The peasants and fisherfolk gathered around Ernesto Cardenal in Solentiname, Nicaragua, had a depth of understanding of the gospel stories that makes much of our thought appear superficial. In my classes at Princeton I was often fascinated by the brilliance of insight of black and women students when I encouraged them to find their own way of thinking and use their own language. As priests and nuns in Latin America enter into the world of the poor and develop a new respect for it, their attitudes toward popular religion and culture have changed dramatically. The culture and religion of the poor are "primitive" only if we assume that ours are advanced and judge theirs by what we have. In reality the creations of the oppressed may represent quite extraordinary achievements, offering them a sense of dignity, creating conditions for a measure of authentic human life in the most degrading circumstances, keeping hope alive, and sustaining visions of a more just society.

We may not have any global solutions to the problem of poverty. But we certainly can change our attitude toward the poor and the world they have created. By honoring their way of life, we remove an oppressive burden we have laid on them; we make it easier for them to accept and affirm what is most authentic for them. As this happens, they find new strength to struggle for their liberation.

This change of attitude can lead to new relationships with those we have until now excluded from our circle of friendship. And we will not need to go very far along this path before realizing how much we have impoverished ourselves by sharing our lives only with people from our own culture and our own social and economic class. Cultural interaction enriches our lives and expands our world.

Whenever a dominant culture is in decline, such interaction is essential for survival. Ongoing contact with those who are the victims of our system will shatter complacency, sharpen our awareness of what is happening around us, and open our eyes to new options that we might not otherwise see for the future. The vision, energy, and passion of those who are fighting for life can inspire us as well. The language and perspective of those who have been kept outside our one-dimensional, technological, and bureaucratic world can help us to break out of our bondage while the quality of interpersonal relationships often developed by the poor for the sake of survival can help save us from the depersonalization we experience in our world of gadgets and techniques.

3. Jesus of Nazareth, the poor Messiah, radically transforms our perception of what is happening in history. For those on top, history is the arena in which those with wealth and power conquer and rule, dominate nature, and exploit the resources of the earth and the labors of the populace to build their great empires. The writers of history tell these stories. They venerate "great" men and women, chronicle their achievements, and extol their virtues.

The Gospels approach history quite differently. They tell the story of events which they claim represent the turning point in history. But these events essentially involve the messianic expectations of the poor and the way they are being realized through the words and deeds of Jesus. Attention is concentrated on the coming kingdom not on a glorified past. The story is about the poor and oppressed and their struggle for life. The "great" and mighty rarely appear in it, and when they do they are the enemy. History is the story of the struggle of the poor to realize their destiny, which is to inherit the earth.

The implications of this are staggering. History is the story of how the people of the world, especially the poor, fulfil their potential as human beings. As Ernst Bloch has said, "What is, cannot be true." As persons we understand who we are only in the light of what we can become as we realize our potential. The same applies to communities, cultures, and nations.

Moreover, what matters in every age and society is what happens in the struggle for liberation: the fragile visions of a more human future, the slowly emerging and often poorly articulated critiques of the status quo, and the precarious and often unsuccessful efforts to move beyond it. In other words, if we dare to claim that Jesus the Messiah offers us the clue to history, then we can hope to have some understanding of history only as we pay attention primarily to those oppressed peoples who hunger and thirst for justice and dare to struggle for it.

Given the present mood in the United States, even to think in these terms is to be out of step with current trends. The protests, radical political movements, and countercultural developments among young people in the sixties are now being discredited and denounced. Their failures are emphasized in order to justify ignoring the issues they raised. The feminist movement is being attacked because of the "harshness" and "excesses" of its pioneers. And a revolution dedicated to achieving justice for the poor in Nicaragua is branded "Marxist-Leninist" and "totalitarian" while U.S. power is being used to destroy it.

From the perspective of the Gospel, these interpretations represent a tragic misreading of history, tragic in part because they deprive us of an opportunity to make sense of what is going on around us and to create a future for ourselves as a nation. Young people in the sixties exposed the evil of a system which, if unchecked, will destroy us all. They dreamed of a more human life and attempted at least to explore some alternatives. Their failure could challenge us to continue in the direction they indicated. Out of the suffering and anger of those women who are most aware of their oppression can come the vision and energy needed to transform relations between women and men for the good of all of us. And when, in the future, the history of Central America is written, the revolutionary struggles now going on there may well be considered of much greater importance than all that the United States is doing in that region.

4. For those underneath the present is intolerable. It represents deprivation and exploitation, suffering and death. When those underneath are not only poor but also Christian, their unwillingness to accept the present order of things can be greatly intensified. The Jesus whom they meet in the Gospels exposes the injustices in the world and declares that his identification with the

poor goes so far that he shares their suffering. He arouses their expectations by declaring that the messianic age is already beginning.

Little wonder that time and again in Christian history groups of poor men and women have been the first to denounce an oppressive order as intolerable and have compelled others to look at it that way. This perception is at the heart of the explosive revolutionary situation in Latin America today. We are by now well aware of its emergence among Roman Catholics. What I discovered during a recent stay in Chile was that some evangelicals are not far behind. Over a period of several weeks I met regularly with a group of Pentecostal pastors. As they began to talk with each other about their situation, gradually their experience of poverty and their intense resentment at the profound humiliation they experienced in Chilean society came to the surface. When they began to relate these newly recognized feelings with their growing awareness of the liberating message of Jesus, I sensed that I was witnessing the emergence of a new social force for change.

Most of us on top look at the present quite differently. We may see and criticize many injustices in it, but we find it *tolerable.* In fact we often develop a remarkable capacity of rationalization in order to make it so. We regret high unemployment, yet we may accept a situation in which more than 10 percent of the working population of our country are denied the one thing our society requires of them to live decently and have a sense of self-worth. We are opposed to racism, but few of us make the effort required to get to know how blacks and Hispanics are humiliated every day in our society, and thus arrive at the point where we too would find our racism intolerable. Those of us who are male declare that we favor the liberation of women, yet again and again the women closest to us lament the fact that we are willing to do something to change our attitudes and ways of relating only when confronted by them.

In addition to this we justify our acceptance of the status quo by convincing ourselves that any possible alternative to it would be worse. In the same breath in which we speak of injustices in capitalism, we declare that socialism would be even more unjust. Our concern to eliminate racism stops at the point where greater racial equality would deprive us of any of our privileges. And our support of the liberation of women is tempered by our fear that they are going too far and will end up establishing the same oppressive patterns we have maintained. The result is that we are immobilized because we have lost the capacity to imagine new solutions—which can only be found beyond the dead ends in which we are caught.

In several of his parables, Jesus announces that the poor and the outcasts are the ones who will sit down at the banquet table of the Messiah. It is they who hunger and thirst after justice and eagerly anticipate the dawning of a new age. Only as those of us on top come to share their perception, their yearning, and their struggle can we also be included. Otherwise, we will end up being passive spectators of a historical struggle from which we have excluded ourselves.

5. For a number of Latin American theologians, a fundamental principle is this: To look at the world and history from above means to be locked into a movement toward death, while to look at the world from below is to be guided by a utopian vision of life. Raúl Vidales, a Mexican theologian, states the case this way: There are two ways to look at history, from the perspective of domination or from the perspective of liberation. The first is antihuman and antiutopian; the second envisions the gradual achievement, in history, of the infinite horizon of another *patria.* One is a theology of death; the other is a theology of life.

Domination leads to death. It condemns the poor to a slow process of death in the midst of life as they are oppressed and deprived of even the bare necessities for life. When the myths that sustain an unjust social system lose their power, that system can survive only as it relies more and more on violence and thus establishes a reign of death. A social order which has no higher goal than self-preservation gradually becomes sclerotic and dies. Even the most intimate human relationships can continue to be lifegiving only as they are re-created time and again. When a couple is content to preserve the relationship they already have, that relationship will soon become sterile and eventually destructive. All social institutions tend to become victims of entropy and move toward inertness. They gradually die—unless they are open to re-creation.

On the other hand the poor, in the midst of death, choose life.

Having nothing, they dream of and yearn for a more human and just society. Having no security in the established order, they can look toward the future, for they have nothing to lose. In this way those who look at the world from underneath keep history open and make life possible for all of us.

For Saint Paul the incredible message of the death and resurrection of Jesus Christ was that we can find new life only as we, individually and collectively, are enabled to die to our past achievements. This, Paul knew, could only be conceived of as foolishness and a scandal by those who were at home in the established order. Thus the God who had acted this way in history for the redemption of human life had to count on those looked upon as foolish—the weak, the lowly, the despised—to be the bearers of this gift to the world (1 Cor. 1:22–28). In one of his most radical declarations at the close of Galatians, he says: "Far be it from me to glory except in the cross of our Lord Jesus Christ, by which the world has been crucified to me, and I to the world. For neither circumcision counts for anything, nor uncircumcision, but a new creation" (6:14–15).

For Eugen Rosenstock-Huessy, a twentieth-century Christian, this means that the great achievement of Jesus was to set us free to bring death into the midst of life so that ultimately we can overcome death; to go against inertia by looking critically at the society we have produced and daring to struggle to transform its very structures. This, according to Rosenstock-Huessy, is the essence of revolutions. For him our modern world is the product of a series of such upheavals, each one brought about by a group or class of persons underneath:

> By realizing the peril of death or decay in time, nations or individuals stem the tide of events. Man is the creature who lifts himself and climbs up-hill; he overcomes the inertia inherent in nature. The waters join the sea; men, in a revolution, flow to the mountain tops and descend on the other side in a new course [Rosenstock-Huessy 1969, 719].

A new encounter with our Christian history will sensitize us to the suffering of the poor and compel us to do something about it. One thing we can do is to enter into their world and begin to look at what is happening around us from their perspective, that is, from below. If we do this we will discover that we soon move beyond any sense of obligation to do something for them. As our perception changes we can see a new opening in our own lives as well. Taking on the cause of the poor is no longer a heavy burden we are obligated to bear. We accept it out of gratitude for the gift we receive from them.

Chapter 6

Changing Values and Changing Sides

CHANGING VALUES AND LIFESTYLES

In Latin America, the discovery of the poor together with the rediscovery of the Gospel has produced radical changes in the lives of many Christians. Priests have left monasteries and nuns have left convents in wealthy sections of a city and have moved to the barrios occupied by the poorest. The houses in which they live do not stand out as better than those around them. They share the life and many of the hardships of the poor. They are there to serve in any way they can. Priests, lawyers, doctors, and teachers have chosen to use their professional training in service of those most in need. And as they have done so, many of them have *changed sides*. The cause of the poor has become their cause; they have shifted their loyalty from the class to which they belonged to solidarity with the dispossessed. This, more than anything else, has aroused the fear and anger of the wealthy and powerful. In one country after another those who have chosen this path have been harassed and persecuted, and some of them have been killed.

Those who have undergone this transformation speak of it as a conversion experience, a "second conversion"—to the poor. As a result of it they have been sensitized to the suffering of those around them and are making what many of us consider to be great sacrifices. But what is communicated when we have contact with them is their tremendous vitality, a strong sense of purpose in life, and a rich experience of personal fulfillment. The number who have chosen this path may be small, but they are in the process of creating a new lifestyle based on a system of values quite in contrast with what we have taken for granted until now.

Sooner or later, we will have to face the challenge they present to us. They raise, for us in the First World as well as for men and women in Latin America, questions about our whole system of values, which defines what is important for us and what gives meaning to our lives. This issue, which has been disturbing many of us for some time, is posed much more sharply by the poor people of the world. They force us to see that to be poor means more than being deprived of the material things most essential to sustain life. *To be poor is to be deprived of everything that our society declares is most important for a human life.* It is to be deprived of that which you and I take for granted as most important. I can have what I consider necessary for a rich and full life only by participating in a system that deprives others of those very things. Consequently the value system which gives life to some makes it intolerable for others.

While living in the South Bronx I had daily contact with young men who had come from Puerto Rico to New York with the expectation that they too could have a share of those things promised by the propaganda of our consumer society. They wanted the same things I or anyone else wants, and they assumed they could get them by following the same track: getting an education, finding a job with the promise of upward mobility, relying on credit and loans. The only problem was that the system that worked for me did not work for them. They never were able to get onto the right track. The school system did not lead them, as it had me, to a college degree. Most of them could find no regular work, let alone jobs with opportunities for advancement. When they depended on credit and loans to get a few things they badly needed, they ended up becoming victims. One after another of them said to me: what comes to you naturally, I can hope to get only illegally.

What happens to many of the elderly is no less disturbing. According to a recent report, in the United States crimes committed by the elderly increased 48 percent from 1978 to 1983, with little or no increase in other age groups during the same period. And two-thirds of the crimes committed by the elderly are violent ones, such as homicide and sexual assault. The situation is alarming but should not surprise us. What we do to older persons is to deprive them, at a certain point in their lives, of the very things they have striven for all their lives, things our society considers essential to happiness: economic well-being, a good job, prestige, and power. From one day to the next all of these things may be taken away from them with no possibility that they will ever be returned. The result, in many cases, is not only serious material deprivation but the loss of any position of respect in society and any sense of self-worth.

For those whose human concern leads them to yearn for a society in which everyone can have a chance for a meaningful life, this problem is an acute one. However for two reasons it cannot be resolved within our present system of values and within the society which implements those values. Firstly, the very things we are taught to value, for which we strive most desperately, without which we cannot be happy, are *scarce*. When we all try to accumulate all the material things we can get, there simply are not enough to go around. For years we harbored the illusion that our advanced technological society would be able to produce enough to overcome poverty and point the way toward a solution for the Third World as well. Now, after we see what the Reagan administration has done to cut back or eliminate programs originally established to provide minimal aid and services to the underprivileged, we are haunted by a quite different question: How many children, elderly women, blacks, and Hispanics will have to be sacrificed in order to maintain our present system of privilege?

If we consider that power and prestige are necessary for us to have a good life, then we face an even greater problem of scarcity. Our society is like a pyramid. These rewards, after which we are taught to strive, are available to us only as we move toward the top. But the higher we go, the fewer the number of positions available. Thus most of us are never able to get what we consider essential for a full human life. If perchance we are among the few who do arrive at the top, we must realize that our achievement deprives others of what we and they most value.

Secondly, our sense of worth is determined by comparing ourselves with other persons. *We value ourselves because we have more than others, are better than others, have climbed higher than others.* We feel good about ourselves to the extent that there are people below us; we are lacking in value to the extent that there are people above us. Consequently we are always threatened by those above us and below us. Competition with others is built into our whole value system.

Add to this the fact that our greatest satisfaction often comes from having power over others. This means that we have to diminish others in order to be ourselves. Our independence is built on making others dependent and denying them the opportunity for self-determination. And as our satisfaction is linked to the dissatisfaction of others, we are always tempted to use our power to defend and preserve what we have. Thus oppression is built into the system. The end result is that the same system which deprives and dehumanizes those on the bottom deprives and dehumanizes those on top as well. The protests of young people in the United States in the sixties were sparked by this discovery. More recently the media reported on large and violent demonstrations in Switzerland in which young people were reacting against the boredom and dehumanization produced by their affluent way of life. As the Latin Americans would put it, the oppressors are also oppressed and need to experience liberation.

Latin American New Testament scholars and the peasants of Solentiname are of one voice when they declare that the life and teachings of Jesus of Nazareth stand in the sharpest contrast to this system of values. If you and I read the Gospels in dialogue with them, we will probably arrive at the same conclusion. But the rational acknowledgment of this fact will not change us. If we take seriously the Latin American experience, a quite different response is called for.

Priests, nuns, and others, after being face to face with the poor, felt themselves compelled to make certain decisions about how they were going to live and work. These decisions created new situations for them in which their values and lifestyles had to be reexamined. This process, in turn, called for new decisions as they came into closer contact with the dispossessed and found themselves involved in social conflict.

At the same time something quite different and unexpected was happening to many of them. Some speak of meeting God in the poor, others of a sort of mystical experience of the presence of Jesus Christ in the lowly. But whether or not they speak in these terms, along this road they have been *addressed* and have received an offer of new life that they could not refuse.

I believe that any breakthroughs on our part will come as we follow a similar process, even though we experience the crisis of values quite differently. We may not yet be ready to respond to the cries of the poor, but some of us are caught in deep internal conflicts in relation to our work. We want it to be personally fulfilling, yet we find that the tasks on which we spend our energies are often boring and without any meaningful connection with the rest of our lives. We would like to use our days making some small contribution to human welfare, yet we often suspect that the organizations and institutions we serve get in the way of our doing this rather than providing an opportunity for it. As these tensions become more acute, a sort of numbness sets in and we settle for less and less.

If, however, we take steps to break out of this impasse, we create a new situation for ourselves and set in motion a process that may be both painful and life-giving. Perhaps as we take such steps, find others who have done the same, and learn from each other, we will discover how our system of values can be transformed for our benefit as well as that of others. Taking this into account I can only speak here of my own limited attempts to do this and reflect briefly on what has happened as a result.

Several years ago, my wife, Nancy, and I found ourselves highly dissatisfied with what we were doing in our professions. I had gone to teach at Princeton Seminary hoping to help prepare a new generation of pastors for leadership in the renewal of the church. But I found myself training professionals for careers in a dying institution. Nancy had created and developed a very successful parenting program at Booth Maternity Center in Philadelphia. While doing so, she realized that what she really wanted to do was to work with parents of small children in poor neighborhoods, providing them with resources which could enable them to develop their capacities for more effective parenting. I finally concluded that I could not, in good conscience, continue as a professor at Princeton and resigned from a position I had held for eighteen years. Some months later Nancy resigned from her position at Booth. By making these decisions, we lost any possibility of identifying who we were in society or what we did by referring to the positions we held. As for income, we had given up two relatively good salaries, according to our standards, and found ourselves with the equivalent of one-half of one salary, provided by a small pension and consulting work offered to us from time to time. In this situation we had no choice but to work at the question of values and lifestyle much more intensely than we had ever done before—with some rather surprising results.

For years I had questioned the attitude of colleagues in academia and the church who would not consider a new job offer unless it gave them a "higher" position and more money. Especially if we have some sense of vocation, why should our decisions about the work we are going to do be so closely tied to social position and income and especially to upward mobility in both areas? When I no longer had any job at all, this question was posed much more radically. I simply had to ask myself what material needs I had and how they could be met. Everything else was quite secondary.

From this perspective a number of things soon became clear. I did not need nearly as much to sustain life as I had earlier thought I did. There were some things I really needed, others I did not. I could discriminate between the two. I could also see that many things I relied on before really got in the way of living more fully. No longer having the money I needed to do what those around me were doing, I began to think about a wider range of possibilities and explore options I had not considered earlier. When we found that we could no longer afford to live in Princeton, we moved to Germantown, where we bought and renovated an old house. As a result we were freed from the burden of a heavy mortgage, had the satisfaction of working together to discover and re-create the beauty of an older house, and, most important of all, our lives were enriched by close contact with people of diverse ethnic and cultural backgrounds living around us.

Somewhat to our surprise we found that we often depended on material things to give a meaning to our lives that they could not provide. We also began to see how often people we knew could relate to each other and to us only around the acquisition and use of material things. The loss of these things helped us to see how superficial many of these satisfactions are and to explore a different quality of relationships.

Strangely enough, at the same time we had begun to value material things more—but in a quite different way than before. To the extent that we were no longer caught up in getting more, we became more aware of what we really needed and attached greater value to it. Faced by the possibility of not being able to pay our bills at the end of the month, we became more sensitive to the plight of those who cannot make ends meet from day to day. And as the acquisition of things lost some of its power over us and the cry of the poor sounded louder in our ears, the struggle to create a more just society took on greater importance. It began to play a more central role in giving meaning to our daily lives.

The question about my system of values was even more sharply raised by my sudden loss of what was considered, in certain circles, to be a prestigious position. As I was trying to figure out what to do with my life, I frequently met people who did not know me. Inevitably they would ask, What are you doing? expecting me, by my answer, to tell them who I was. And time and again I would catch myself beginning an answer to their question by saying, "Well, for the last eighteen years I've been teaching at Princeton."

I gradually came to see that, by this response, I was saying that my sense of my own worth and of what I had accomplished with my life was tied up with that position. Why was this the case? Could I feel good about myself only if I stood out over others? If these were really the values by which I functioned, then much of my preaching had been quite hypocritical. I had declared, over and over again, that in Christ, God had demonstrated love for us and had forgiven and accepted us. This is the foundation for our sense of our own worth. We are affirmed and valued by God; we have been freed from the compulsion to prove our worth—to ourselves or others—in other ways. I had to admit to myself that I did not live by this doctrine and, also, that my recognition of that fact did not change my situation.

And yet it was precisely this experience of being affirmed, accepted, and valued—in a rich love relationship—that began to turn my values around and helped me to see how deprived I had been until that time. I began to explore a wider range of possibilities for personal growth and development and thus to discover that, once our most basic material needs are met, *becoming* is more important than *having*. I soon began to suspect that for many of us our struggle for power, prestige, and money represents a futile attempt to overcome the emptiness and barrenness of our personal lives.

Finding myself no longer cast in a professional *role*, I came to perceive how many of our relationships to other people are really superficial role-to-role relationships. The role becomes a strait jacket. If we succeed in going beyond it, we can listen to, share with, and become vulnerable to others and thus find a new quality of relationships. If we are then able to reach out to those of other races, classes, and cultures, this new quality of relationship has almost unlimited possibilities of expansion, bringing greater richness to our otherwise deprived lives. In this context we realize that competition diminishes life; cooperation enhances it. Human fulfillment comes as we receive gifts that enrich and expand our lives and as we learn to give as well.

In earlier years I felt an *obligation* to serve others, to do something socially significant. That responsibility often became burdensome, leaving me exhausted. Now I experience something quite different. A new richness of personal life and a new quality of interpersonal relationships provide energy for social involvement and sustain it. In fact, a life of this sort can only find fulfillment in the struggle to provide others with the opportunity to have a fuller life.

Saint Augustine spoke of the fundamental conflict between the orders of this world and the kingdom of God as that between "the love of power and the power of love." For us today this means something very specific: *The love of power* is the will to have power over other women and men, to exploit them, suppress them, and keep them in inferior positions so that we can have the life we want; *the power of love* is the quality of relationship through which we empower each other and thus create conditions for those underneath and for ourselves to have a full life, as all of us become subjects of our own lives and destinies.

This, I believe, is at the heart of a Christian social vision for our time. The test of the vitality of Christian faith will be its power to transform human life in this direction. The theologians of the fourth century argued that Christians were not engaged in imposing alien values on the world and human life. Rather, their faith enabled them to perceive what was really there. I would claim that when we attempt today to raise up mutual empowerment—in contrast to the will to power—as the road to a full life, we are doing something similar. If only we are free to follow this route, we may find it much more rewarding than the constant struggle for power, which is as prevalent within the family and in all our institutions at all levels as it is at the top of the economic and political pyramids. As I look back now on my experience as a teacher, I have no doubt that my most rewarding experiences were those in which I helped students discover their own potential, think for themselves, and find their own way.

We may be overwhelmed by the suffering of such vast numbers of poor persons in our world today. We may also feel frustrated by our inability to find effective means to bring about change in their situation. But we can be sure of one thing: *Fundamental changes can come about only as we undergo a radical transformation in our system of values.* That is a task in which we can all be engaged right now.

Today many of those in positions of affluence look to the future with apprehension. All that they can see ahead of them and their children is the loss of much of what they have and cherish. I have a very different idea of what lies ahead of us. If this present crisis can become the occasion for a fundamental change in values, we can look toward a future in which a much higher degree of human fulfillment will be possible for a larger percentage of the world's population. If and when that happens, future generations will look back upon this age and describe it as a time of human underdevelopment, an age of barbarism in which our struggles for fulfillment by means of domination over others took a very heavy toll. By this I do not mean that future generations will have overcome the evils caused by the struggle for power. That will take new forms, and they will be judged by their capacity to deal with these manifestations of evil. The judgment history will pass on us is that we not only accepted but gave the highest value to a way of life based upon love of power, which ended up dehumanizing us as well as those we exploited.

THE SIDE OF THE POOR

Most of the Latin Americans I have known who heard the cry of the poor never imagined, at the beginning, that it would lead them to abandon their own social class and change sides. But this is what has happened to many of them. And it was not the poor but rather their own class—those in power—who drove them to this decision.

I think of Paulo, with whom I was closely associated for a number of years in Brazil. When I first met him, he had just graduated from the university. From our first meeting what most impressed me was his extraordinary sensitivity to the suffering of needy persons. Every time we walked down the street, he would stop to talk with every beggar who approached him and usually ended up without any money in his pockets. When the Christian Student Movement began a mission in a poor neighborhood, Paulo was one of the first to go there to live. As he became aware of what was happening to the factory workers among whom he lived, he turned his attention to efforts to organize them. Later he returned to his home state and began to help fisherfolk organize small cooperatives to purchase what they needed and sell their fish directly to the consumer. Eventually he became involved in politics and was elected to the state legislature.

As I recall our conversations over several years, one thing stands out: every attempt Paulo made to help the poor help themselves was attacked by those in power; the more successful these efforts became, the more violent the reaction against them. This led him gradually to perceive that Brazilian society was divided into classes, that the struggle of the poor meant class conflict, and that, in this situation, he had to change sides. In his conversations with those of us closest to him, this question came more and more to the fore, and he frequently challenged us to be clear about which side we were on. After the military coup in 1964, Paulo was removed from the legislature. Later on he was arrested and "disappeared" in prison, never to be heard from again.

For Paulo, as for many others, the turning point came when they realized that the struggle of the poor would inevitably lead to class conflict. Loyalty to the poor therefore meant being disloyal to one's own class. Sharing the struggle of the poor meant working against the continued domination and exploitation by which that class lived.

In one country after another the wealthy and powerful have been the first to draw these lines. A seminarian, a young doctor, or a social worker may go to a poor neighborhood to be of service, often without any clearly articulated political position. But such an act may be, in itself, reason enough for them to be arrested, tortured, and even killed.

I recall the story one pastor told me. He had worked with the poor for many years. But he never felt that he had done enough to share their poverty or support their cause. In fact he was never quite clear in his own mind as to which side he was really on. And then there was a military takeover in his country, and he was among the first to be arrested. During the months he spent in prison, it dawned on him that if he didn't know for sure on which side he stood, those in power did.

When Christians in Latin America speak of a "second conversion," they speak out of this history. Those whose loyalties are divided will be immobilized and rendered ineffective. But if they show real concern for the poor, they will not be spared. In these situations Jesus' radical call to discipleship and Saint Paul's assertion that we must die to our past in order to find new life in Christ are heard with unusual clarity. Conversion implies a clear break with the values, loyalties, and goals of the class to which one formerly belonged and the resultant freedom to identify fully with the struggle of the dispossessed. It means changing sides. This revolutionary shift is one of the major sources of the vitality and power of Christian movements for social change in Latin America today.

Does all this have any relevance to the situation of those of us who live in the First World? Our efforts to help the dispossessed aren't blocked nor do they usually lead to class war. Our involvement in one form or another of social and political action doesn't usually end up with our being viciously attacked or marked for elimination. And the very idea of being forced to choose sides in a social conflict between the rich and the poor, especially if that means that we stand with the poor against our own class, is repugnant to us. Even in our most liberal circles, we are content to concentrate our primary attention on the pursuit of our own personal interests and do what we can on the side to help those who happen to be less fortunate than we are.

In my association with Latin American Christians, however, I find that their witness disturbs my tranquility at this point. They attune my ears to a gospel that declares that my religious quest for meaning in life and for transcendence must lead me toward the poor. If I enter into their world and listen to their cry from this perspective, then the struggle to create conditions for a decent life for the poor and the empowerment of the powerless becomes my *primary* concern. To take this seriously calls for solidarity with those who are the victims of the established order. Even my timid efforts to follow this path suggest to me that for several reasons this means changing sides.

1. As long as I relate to the situation of the poor as a detached observer, I can easily assess the relative merits of both sides and continue to be at ease on the side on which I find myself. If I try to be of some service to them in my spare time, the same holds true. But the moment I consider loving my neighbors as myself—that is, becoming as concerned about their well-being as I am about my own—then the whole scene changes. The well-being of the oppressed depends upon overcoming their situation of oppression. If I, who benefit from an oppressive system, want to do anything for the victims of it, the decision to change sides is my starting point.

This is something I find that the oppressed understand very clearly. The moment they overcome their sense of inferiority, realize that they cannot and will not depend on those over them to rescue them, and take on the responsibility for their own liberation, they demand one thing of those who want to do anything to help them: *that they change sides.*

Many years ago, in Latin America, I was forced to face this fact. When I came to realize what my country was doing to exploit the people in that part of the world and watched as the government of the United States intervened in one country after another to help overthrow more progressive regimes, I reacted in a number of ways. At times I tried to explain and defend, to some extent, what the United States was doing. At others, I tried to apologize. As a U.S. citizen, I was often overwhelmed by a sense of guilt. And then I came to see that for my Latin American friends and colleagues only one thing really mattered. Where did I stand? Which side was I on? For them the situation called for a clear decision, on their part and on mine. They assumed that I, even though a U.S. citizen, could see what was happening and take a stand for justice. But until I arrived at that point, I could make no contribution to that struggle.

In more recent years my attempts to deal with racism in the United States have led me to the same conclusion. Living and working with blacks and Hispanics, I began to realize what racial prejudice has done to them over the generations. I have at least some understanding of why they perceive racism to be the supreme evil, why their anger can be so intense, and how much they have been forced to suffer because of it. And I cannot escape the fact that I belong to the segment of the population that has perpetrated all this, that I profit from it, and that those who belong to other racial groups are well aware of that fact.

At the same time, in the midst of it all, the blacks and Hispanics with whom I am associated assume that I am, above all else, a human being capable of comprehending the injustices that whites have perpetrated, of refusing to accept this situation, and of doing all I can to overcome it. But they also make it abundantly clear to me that I can share in their struggle with them only by changing sides. This, for them, is the supreme test of my commitment.

2. This witness of the oppressed is confirmed by my own experience working for change within some of our major institutions. At Princeton I found many students who were dissatisfied and frustrated with the way the seminary functioned. They definitely felt oppressed by the institution. But with greater awareness of their situation came greater depression. By and large they were immobilized. For they were products of the institutions which oppressed them. They were rebels who were, at the same time, tied by past loyalties and future expectations to the institutions they condemned.

Several of my colleagues felt this contradiction even more acutely. They understood very well how the institution worked against the things they most valued. But their efforts to work for change were limited by their adherence to the rules of the game, which kept the existing system going. In my case I found that I was free to speak and act from a radical, critical perspective—as long as it was clear that I was loyal to the institution and played the game by the established rules. Those who ran the seminary understood much better than I did that my presence there was no serious threat under these conditions. But when I decided to change sides—that is, to join forces with those who were trying to find a way to bring about fundamental structural changes and build a base for that struggle—doors quickly closed in front of me, and I found myself increasingly isolated and ostracized. Frequently those who attacked me most vigorously were those who shared my analysis of what was wrong but were not willing to make this break. Since that happened, I have been amazed to find many other women and men who have had the same experience when they took a similar stand in government, business, or other organizations.

3. Those of us concerned about social injustice in the United States and the rest of the First World have been able to avoid changing sides because we believed that injustices were being overcome and that our society was open and thus capable of further transformation. We may not be able to sustain this belief much longer. The closer our contact with the poor, the more evident it will be that they have been abandoned by those in power, that their number is increasing, and that they are getting poorer. Even a long-term economic recovery may not improve their situation significantly and in the United States will probably leave a high percentage of blacks and Hispanics, especially the young, as well as women and elderly persons permanently unemployed.

Moreover, as the crisis of society in the First World deepens, resistance to change grows, especially among those in power whose positions are most threatened by it. Attempts are now being made to discredit the peace movement by denouncing it as influenced by the Soviets. The mass media are accused of deceiving the public when they portray honestly what is happening in Central America, and the time may soon come when those in the United States who vigorously oppose their country's policy there will be declared traitors. As this happens, those who portray realistically what is happening to the poor at home and abroad and try to work effectively for change should not be surprised if steps are taken to stop them. Under such circumstances we will be better able to understand why changing sides is of such great importance.

In the highly polarized situation in much of Latin America, changing sides is something that often happens very quickly. For many of us in the First World, it is more likely to be the result of a long process. As a first step, many of us will have to reach out to the outcasts and the powerless, the deprived and exploited; get to know them and enter their world; share some of their pain and become involved with them in their daily struggles. This may involve a change of place of residence, joining another church, or working professionally with grassroots organizations in the ghetto. As a result of such contacts and the new relationships developing around them, we may find ourselves moving to a new level of commitment to their struggle and recognizing that this struggle is our own as well. For us as for many Latin Americans, this may lead to a "second conversion," through which we are set free from divided loyalties and discover new sources of energy. As a result of this conversion experience, our new freedom to be loyal to the cause of those underneath will gradually break the power over us of former loyalties and allow us to struggle for justice even when that involves working against the interests of the class to which we have belonged.

This decision will free us for new involvements. It will also create new problems for us, especially if our efforts are to any degree successful. Finding ourselves under attack, marginalized, and perhaps persecuted, we will be able to live out our new commitments to the poor only if we can understand how the system opposed to us is functioning, be guided by the vision of an alternative economic and political order, and develop a community of support among the poor and those who stand with them. We may not have—nor do we need to have at present—any blueprints for action capable of bringing about the changes we consider most imperative. But we will be called upon to have a sophisticated analysis of our society and of the contradictions in it; we will also have to be much more daring in our thinking about a new economic order as well as in proposing and experimenting with new solutions.

Chapter 7

A Decent Life for the Poor

TOWARD A NEW ECONOMIC ORDER IN POOR NATIONS

When I first began to read the history of missions in Africa, I was struck by comments frequently made by European colonial administrators who were attempting to contain the early movements for independence and blamed the missionaries for sowing the seeds of the desire for freedom. Years later I met a number of leaders of African independence movements. They often spoke of their participation in Bible study groups in mission schools. It was there that they began to dream of freedom and decided that the colonial system had to go. Today, in Latin America at least, this process has gone one step further. As poor people have come together to study the Bible, they have begun to dream of economic justice and have decided that this means the end of the capitalist system as they have known it.

Some of the young African Christians with whom I spoke met secretly to study the Bible because they could not look to their missionary teachers for support. Now, in Latin America, Roman Catholic bishops are often the ones who are boldly encouraging the poor. In the northeast of Brazil, for example, the bishops' consciences have been deeply troubled by what is occurring in that region: the ruthless exploitation of the peasants, the number of persons who die of starvation or barely survive, and the violence to which the peasants are subjected when they try to do anything to change their situation. In the midst of this suffering, these bishops are calling for a radically different economic order. In a statement issued in 1973, "Marginalização de um povo" (The Marginalization of a People), they declare:

> We want to see a world in which the fruits of work will belong to all. We want to see a world in which people will work, not in order to get rich, but in order that all should possess the necessities of life: enough to eat for their health, a house, education, clothes, shoes, water, and light. We want to see a world in which money is placed at the service of human beings and not human beings at the service of money. We want to see a world in which all will be able to work for all, not a divided world in which all persons work only for themselves. Therefore, we want to see a world in which there will be only one people with no division between rich and poor.

There is nothing particularly new in this vision of a better future for the poor. What is new here is the conviction that capitalism is the major obstacle to the realization of this dream: "We have to overcome capitalism, this is the greater evil, . . . the tree that produces the fruits we know: poverty, hunger, destitution, death for the great majority." For an increasing number of concerned Christians in Latin America, the private ownership of the means of production—dominated by multinational corporations and oriented toward one goal, *profit*—now stands out as the enemy. Especially when economic power is closely allied with repressive political regimes in the national security state, economic development means that those on top get richer while the masses get poorer. The poor are used, when needed, in the productive process; otherwise the system ignores them or works against them. They are marginalized economically and politically, and when they try to do anything about it, their movements are destroyed, with brutal force if necessary. But by following this road, the established order is producing its own gravediggers, and included among them are many Christians of conscience.

This new awareness places a heavy burden on Christians and any others who want to see justice done to the poor. They have the responsibility to analyze how the present economic system operates and why it is the enemy of the people. They have to come up with an alternative economic order and show how it could deal more effectively with the tough realities of underdevelopment and the poverty accompanying it. And they are required to offer some reasonable hope that the changes called for can be brought about.

In these areas the theologians of liberation have already accomplished a great deal as they have succeeded not only in bringing together economists, sociologists, political scientists, and theologians to work on these problems, but also in joining with the poor and listening to them.

I first became aware of the range and quality of their work when I attended a conference of social scientists and theologians in San José, Costa Rica, in 1978. What most impressed me was not only the quality of the papers presented and the richness of the discussion but also the fact that most of those attending the conference were associated with study and research centers—located all over Central and South America—in which theologians and social scientists were working together on these problems. To cite only one example, one of those present was Xabier Gorostiaga, a Jesuit priest who is trained both in theology and economics. At that time he was working with a small team in Panama. Later he occupied a position in the Ministry of Planning of the revolutionary government in Nicaragua. More recently he resigned from that position in order to organize and direct the Institute for Economic and Social Research. This institute, in the short time it has been functioning, has not only succeeded in forming a network of scholars who are working throughout Central America on alternative projects for economic development of that region, but it is also drawing on research being done in the United States which can be of help to them in their efforts.

As theologians and social scientists have joined with other men and women in study and research from Mexico to Chile, their thought has moved along several lines, on which by now there is an emerging consensus, which many of us in the First World may not find easy to understand or accept.

1. In their attempt to understand and change their societies, Latin Americans are drawing on the thought of Karl Marx and on Marxist categories in much the same way that many First World

Christians draw on the thought of Sigmund Freud and psychoanalytic language to understand and help those whom they are counseling.

For the poor and those concerned about their poverty, it is imperative to understand how the present society functions: how the economic system operates and why; who has power and how it is used. In other words, it is absolutely necessary to analyze the structures of oppression and perceive clearly what they are doing to people. Especially when young people become aware of the need to do this and find that the liberal social thought they have been taught fails them at this point, the discovery of Marx can be exciting. Here they find a body of thought that deals precisely with these issues, opens up new perspectives, and provides them with tools to analyze their society.

With the help of Marx, they are able to see more clearly the contradictions in their society, think in terms of a process of systemic change, and envision an alternative to the present order. The language of class struggle, with the emphasis on two groups having different interests, makes sense in countries in which a few have power and privilege and use the system they have established to deprive the great majority of both. And wherever the major political parties all work together to maintain the status quo, what Marx has to say about the proletariat and its role in the transformation of society focuses attention on the poor and on new political forces emerging from the masses.

For many Christians this discovery of Marx has an added dimension. It forces them to recognize elements in their Christian faith to which they previously had been blind—for instance, the fact that the God of the Bible is active in the concrete social and political realities of historical existence, the central concern for social justice in the Old Testament prophets, and the emphasis on the transformation of life and history. In the words of Gustavo Gutiérrez, "it is to a large extent due to Marxism's influence that theological thought, searching for its own sources, has begun to reflect on the meaning of the transformation of this world and the action of God in history" (Gutiérrez 1973, 9).

When Christians in the First World become excited about the new insights they are gaining from psychoanalytic language, we may rightly want them to take a more critical look at it. But it hardly occurs to us to denounce them as "Freudists" or to attack them and question their Christian commitment because they draw on these categories. I see no reason why we should not adopt a similar stance in relation to Latin American Christians who draw on Marx and Marxian thought in the same way.

2. As capitalism produces ever greater inequality and relies more on repression, the option for socialism gains ground among Christians. As the word is more widely used, it also becomes clear that it means many different things to different people and groups. Some would emphasize more than others the differences between their type of socialism and the new order envisioned by the Marxists. All would insist that only the social ownership of the means of production will make it possible to meet the needs of the great majority of Latin Americans but there are many diverse ideas as to specifically what this will mean. Moreover, one of the major characteristics of this movement toward socialism on the part of Christians is an emphasis on learning in the midst of the struggle and working out concrete solutions to specific problems, rather than confiding in doctrinaire conceptual systems and blueprints.

We in the First World will be able to understand and have a fruitful dialogue with our sisters and brothers in Latin America only if we have some idea of what this major shift toward socialism means for them.

We start out from a position of relative affluence in an established order from which we profit. From that position we assume that socialism will not work and that it will inevitably lead to a totalitarian society. This assumption may not be true, but most of us are not highly motivated to critically analyze it. The starting point for Latin Americans is a very different one: the system they have at present has not met and cannot meet the needs of the great majority of persons; it isn't working. The imperative they face is to try to create a different economic order that will meet these human needs. For them socialism represents that alternative.

Moreover, when they look at socialism from this perspective, they see something else: some of the major goals of socialism are very much in line with their own Christian values. One group of bishops has stated that it finds, at the origins of socialism, "an aspiration to justice, a desire to improve the condition of the poor, a will to control the power of money, and a desire for equality.'' These, they say, are Christian values to be found in the Bible and the Gospels. They are "our values, which cannot be denied merely because others take them as theirs" (cited in Lesbaupin).

In many situations of underdevelopment, the model that has been pushed by the United States no longer makes sense. What socialism proposes does. It seems very reasonable to develop an economic system which will start with the resources of human beings, raw materials, and technology available in a particular country and use them to meet the most fundamental needs of all the persons in that country. Poor nations that are becoming poorer and more dependent as they are integrated into the international economic order serving primarily the interests of the United States and multinational corporations may find a socialist alternative very appealing. It makes sense to them to build their economy around the resources they have to meet their basic needs, and as they do so, to see how they can join with other poor countries striving to help each other. And societies in which the great majority of persons are poor can become democratic only as the economic order contributes to their well-being.

Many Christians who espouse socialism look critically at the socialist regimes that have been established thus far. They consider it important to learn from the failures as well as the successes of these experiments, especially in the Third World. But they insist that our assessment of socialism should not be determined by the limitations of what now exists. For them, socialism is an open-ended "project": it is in the process of development. Its full historical potential is still far from being realized. For this reason it is important to allow a new social order to evolve as specific problems are tackled and proposed solutions are tried out. A clear sense of direction is necessary, but reliance on closed conceptual schemes and blueprints is to be avoided.

I am convinced that much of the optimism about socialism is due to the new relationship developing between Christians and Marxists. By now both groups know that a socialist society can be created only if they work together. This is certainly not easy. But as they turn their attention away from the intellectual confrontation of two ideological systems toward interaction with each other in the midst of their common identification with the poor and participation in their struggle, many on both sides are being changed.

Both groups are finding that their abstract conceptual systems and arguments mean little to the poor; at the same time they are often amazed by the richness of insight and wisdom of the poor, from whom they are beginning to learn. As they share the poverty and see the tremendous sacrifices being made by the poor, their commitment to building a future society in which these people will have life and power is deepened. As this happens, many Christians and Marxists find that they not only share a common vision and commitment but that they are learning from and supporting each other. There are, to be sure, Marxists who are rigid and doctrinaire and whose human sensitivities have been dulled in the struggle for power. But then women and men who daily run up against Christians who function in this same way have learned that fundamentalism's perversion of certain aspects of Christianity is not sufficient reason to categorically reject Christianity and the contributions it can make. Why then should Marxism be categorically judged on the basis of the words and actions of certain rigid and doctrinaire Marxists?

3. This involvement of Christians and Marxists with the dispossessed and the ensuing interaction between the two groups may provide a new model for development of the poorest countries and a new hope for their people. Beginning with the revolution in Nicaragua, we have a possibility for the emergence of a social and economic order which will go beyond the achievements of the earlier Marxist societies in the Third World and also provide an alternative to the model offered—and often imposed—by the First World.

In Nicaragua intense concern to improve the lot of the poor has led to the search for pragmatic solutions rather than the imposition of dogmatic answers. For example, Nicaragua has established a mixed economy, in which approximately 60 percent of industrial production is in the hands of the private sector; also, a high level of agricultural production is maintained by combining the formation of farm cooperatives, the redistribution of land to single families, and state ownership of sugar and other large plantations.

The fact that before the revolution the poor represented such a large percentage of the population and the politico-economic elite was so small has opened the way for advances in popular democracy after the revolution. This very small elite has resented the loss of political power commensurate with its economic power but has little popular support. Thus the United States finds itself in a most anomalous position. In El Salvador, the United States supports militarily a regime that has so little popular support that it has to massacre tens of thousands of its citizens to stay in power. At the same time, the United States attempts to destroy a regime in Nicaragua that enjoys widespread support from the masses and thus offers a sound basis for popular participation in a democratic process never before seen in Latin America.

Most important of all, the awakening of the poor, the development of the basic ecclesial communities, and the widespread efforts at popular education on the part of the church and some political movements are creating conditions for a new society in which the poor will occupy a position they never held before. The crucial issue is not how to do something for the poor but how to empower them and provide them with ever increasing opportunities to build a more just and egalitarian society. Many Christians and Marxists share this vision and see it as constituting the major challenge to both of their movements in the years ahead. What has happened in Nicaragua strengthens their belief that such a social order can be built.

TOWARD A NEW ECONOMIC ORDER
IN THE UNITED STATES

In the sixties, I came to the conclusion that this changing attitude of Christians toward Marxism and socialism made a great deal of sense in Latin America. As I have observed how this has continued to evolve, my hope for the future of the people of Latin America has been renewed. I now believe that these countries can find ways to develop their economies that will lead to greater material well-being for the poor at the same time that they develop political structures in which power is exercised from below. But I did not believe that all this was relevant to the United States and thus made little effort to bring the thought of the theologians of liberation to the attention of North Americans. Three recent developments have led me to change my mind.

1. *What the United States is doing in Central America and other parts of the Third World.* Our present policies spell disaster for many Third World countries and will eventually prove destructive for us as well.

On the basis of what I have seen in Nicaragua, I have concluded that it is in the national interest of the United States to support the Sandinista revolutionary regime. The Sandinistas overthrew a regime that served the interests of the members of one family and their cronies who together had devastated the economy and had relied more and more on violence to repress an exploited people. A new economic order is developing that is aimed at producing food for the poor and providing them with housing and health care. A national literacy campaign has been followed by the extension of opportunities for education to a wide circle of children and adults. The people, especially the young and the poor, no longer live in fear and are finding opportunities they never had before to participate in the exercise of political power. The leaders with whom I spoke, whether Christian or Marxist, had the same goal: to move in the direction of political and economic independence in order to find their own solutions to their own problems.

What the United States is now doing, however, is quite the opposite. We are the aggressors, supporting efforts to destroy this regime. We are doing so by training and arming primarily members of the Somocista National Guard, who were responsible for sustaining the exploitation and barbarism of the previous regime. If these people were to return to power, the efforts now being made toward justice and democracy would be wiped out; those now working to create a new society would be brutally attacked, killed, or exiled. And the United States would be stuck in one more impossible situation.

In El Salvador, on the other hand, we have intervened militarily to support those who have neither the will nor the capacity to create a democratic society or to develop an economic order serving the needs of the people. They can hope to remain in power only through a reign of terror in which thousands are being tortured and killed. And as their situation inevitably deteriorates, the United States becomes more involved in sustaining this state of affairs.

Moreover, these are not isolated events. U.S. policy is doing the same thing elsewhere in Latin America, in the Philippines, in

South Korea, and in other Third World countries. As I keep asking myself why this is happening, the only conclusion I can reach is that we are victims of an ideology and an economic system that can function only to serve our narrow interests at the expense of the rest of the world. We assume that we have the right of access to the riches and raw materials of the poor countries, but we give them no equal right of access to our rich agricultural resources. We insist on the freedom for multinational corporations to exploit the human and material resources of poor countries and thus seem willing to go to almost any length to stop independent economic development outside that system of exploitation. We talk about freedom and democracy, and yet we support the most unjust and repressive regimes as long as they fit into our international economic schemes. David Rockefeller, for example, went to Argentina in 1977 at the height of the "disappearances" and commented: "I have the impression that finally Argentina has a regime that understands the private enterprise system." In the face of all this, many Christians I know in the Third World who are concerned about justice to the poor have concluded that the United States is becoming more and more involved in a war against the poor of the world. Why can we not see this, ask ourselves why it is happening, and take steps to change our policy?

2. *What I see happening around me in the United States.* I am not an economist nor have I done extensive research on the conditions under which the poor live. But as I find myself in closer contact with the underprivileged, I realize that our economic system serves well the interests of some groups while failing to take the interest of others into account.

In poor Third World countries, external economic and political forces, allied with a small elite within each country, control the economy and exploit it to serve their purposes. The needs and interests of the majority are largely ignored, and they have little or no control over what is happening. My experience in North Philadelphia and the South Bronx indicates that poor blacks and Hispanics are in the same situation in this country. In other words, we have a "Third World" within our nation as well. The economic and political life of the ghetto is controlled by outside forces for their advantage. Unemployment, especially among young men, is much higher than the national average. Very little is being done by government or private foundations to provide financial assistance for the development of local business and industry. And those who are deprived and powerless see themselves as victims of a system working against them. A Baptist minister who has lived and worked in one of these areas for many years recently said to me: "Here, for the first time, the young men have neither jobs nor hope."

Other groups—the young, the elderly, and women—are in a somewhat similar situation in our society today. To some extent, at least, many persons in each of these segments of our population can claim that our economic system does not function to serve their interests. They may or may not benefit personally from it, but they cannot rely on it to take their collective needs into account.

The ways in which the Reagan administration is responding to the present crisis raises for me further questions along this same line. With unemployment having climbed to around 10 percent (not counting those who have given up hope of finding a job), I find profoundly disturbing the ease with which government officials and others accept a high level of unemployment as tolerable, as long as the economy is able to pull out of the recession. These people may be aware of the devastating effects of this situation on those who cannot find work and on their families, but I see little evidence that they are willing to take decisive steps to do something about it. The drastic cuts over the last few years from social programs on which the poor have depended for subsistence have not occurred because our economy is incapable of meeting their most elementary needs. The cuts have taken place at the same time that changes in the federal tax structure and the undoing of the apparatus by which government regulates business are promoting what Frances Fox Piven and Richard Cloward call a "massive upward redistribution of income" (Piven and Cloward 1982, 7). What we have here, according to them, is "a new class war on the unemployed, the unemployable, and the working poor" (p. 1).

Whether or not these conclusions are entirely justified, the Christian conscience, sensitized to the poor, is under the obligation to be in close touch with their deprivation and suffering, to try to understand better why this is happening, and at least to face the possibility that such injustices may be inherent in our economic system.

3. *Persistent questions about the dehumanizing elements in our society.* From what I have seen in Latin America and in the United States, I am more and more convinced that in capitalism we human beings have created an economic order that is not human, in which human well-being is not of primary importance. Karl Marx brought this to the attention of the world and labeled it "exploitation." But for him this exploitation had to do with wages and profits. What we can now see is that a change in the ownership of the means of production does not come to grips with some of the major threats to a full human life, such as, bureaucratic state control or the violation of the natural environment.

Eugen Rosenstock-Huessy goes beyond Marx in his analysis of the causes of this dehumanization. In *Out of Revolution* he claims that the tremendous success of capitalism has been possible because it refuses to take responsibility for the worker as a human being, for the social order of which the individual is a part, or for the renovation and re-creation of society. The "curse of capitalism," he says, lies in "the irresponsibility of the employer for the *reproduction* of the forces he hires, uses, and eventually destroys or wastes" (Rosenstock-Huessy 1969, 87).

Whatever the extent of exploitation and injustice in precapitalist societies, employers owed security to their employees. The lord of the manor fed his workers and their families all the year round; landlord and tenant continuously were dependent upon each other. But with the emergence of the market economy, oriented exclusively to the production of things to be sold as cheaply as possible, all this changed. Entrepreneurs can compete in this market only if they buy the services of the workers by the hour. Employers deal with a labor force to be purchased for specific periods of time. Their responsibility to those *persons* does not extend beyond this transaction. The rhythm of the workers' lives and their past and future are of no concern, and consequently what the workers do on the job has little connection with the wider range of experiences that give meaning to human life. They work at a job in order to make money.

Moreover, a system which cannot be concerned about the full life of the worker, about the rhythm of that life, or about its future takes even less responsibility for society as a whole. Education, the preservation of order, and medical care are by and large left to the government, as is concern about pollution of the atmosphere and destruction of the environment. Industrialization disrupts traditional societies and communities and creates enormous social problems, which can be solved only as new responses are imagined and worked out. This, according to Rosenstock-Huessy, is the ultimate test, and this is where capitalism fails: "Capitalism can make profits only so long as it can escape the cost of reproducing the political and social order" (p. 89).

In advanced industrial societies, progressive political forces together with organized labor have little success when they try to hold the large corporations responsible for the social problems they create. Especially in times of economic crisis, when these corporations are facing strong international competition, they use their political power to reduce taxes and weaken government regulations. In this way they take even less responsibility for the problems they create. They bring pressure on the workforce to surrender gains already made or move to areas of the country where the workers are not organized. And they extend their reach into underdeveloped countries where they bear no responsibility for the social and political order and where they can compete easily with precapitalistic modes of production in more traditional societies. Along this road, in both the underdeveloped and advanced industrial societies, the human cost increases from year to year.

If we are willing to face some of these critical questions, what the Latin Americans are saying and doing may not turn out to be so outrageous after all. In fact we may discover that they and the other poor persons of the world are offering *us* a chance to break free from our ideological bondage and have a future of greater promise. The gospel, mediated through them, can become for us the good news that our salvation is not tied to the maintenance of an economic system in which the striving for wealth and power impoverishes and dehumanizes so many. Rather, we as a nation will have a future as we strive to establish an economic order, here at home and around the world, in which the powerful and the marginalized can join together to develop the resources of the earth so that all may have life.

That future can be ours only if a significant number of women and men in our society become passionately committed to working for fundamental changes in our economic system. My experience in Latin America has shown me that this can happen and that small groups of Christians can play an important part in it. What we need in order to do it is not a blueprint for a new economic order but a new vision of the future, a willingness to join others in finding ways to live and act more in line with that vision and thus to participate effectively in a difficult and dangerous struggle. When I try to relate what I have learned from Latin Americans to the situation in the United States, several things stand out.

From a Christian perspective, we should rejoice in the attention now being given by some economists and others to the importance of "moral" and "spiritual" factors in our economic development. This has been stated most vigorously by George Gilder in *Wealth and Poverty*, a book acclaimed by David Stockman and other members of the Reagan administration. In it the author laments that economists so often fail to emphasize such things as "high adventure and redemptive morality." Our economy, he says, can function only if it has a moral base. We cannot have a free society unless people have reason to believe that it is also a just society. Dynamic economic development depends upon the maintenance of a spirit of adventure, upon creativity and innovation, which alone can overcome the "laws of deterioration and decay" (Gilder 1981, 260). The world is pregnant with doom without "love and faith that infuse ideas with life and fire" (p. 262).

For Gilder all this serves to provide a rationale for supply-side economics and for a new defense of unregulated capitalism. At this point Gilder would have done well to probe a bit more deeply into the religious heritage he exalts. Reinhold Niebuhr, whom he quotes at the end of his last chapter, and other ethicists remind us of the ways those in positions of power and wealth deceive themselves and distort reality to justify their position. Gilder conveniently ignores the attitude expressed in the Gospels toward the poor. It is precisely awareness of this attitude that has led many Latin American Christians—in contrast with Gilder—to stand with the poor and join their struggle. In this way they find that the gospel transforms their perception of what is happening around them as well as their sense of what is involved in moral and spiritual responsibility.

When they share the life of the poor, they can no longer have illusions about the justice of the present system. When they join the poor in their struggle for justice, they find themselves caught up in an adventure which is innovative and creative, the struggle for a more egalitarian society. And they realize that nothing indicates more clearly the bankruptcy of the established order than its inability to imagine and work for alternatives capable of meeting the needs of the dispossessed.

This, I believe, will also be the crucial test for us in the United States in the years ahead. In early 1982 I made a trip to Nicaragua at a time when the devastating impact on the poor of the federal cuts in social programs in the United States was beginning to be felt. At that time I was disturbed to see how incapable our political leaders were of inventing and fighting for alternative solutions and how immobilized so many of the poor were because they had lost hope. In contrast, in Nicaragua I was amazed to sense the vitality, energy, and hard work of those who were caught up in the adventure to create a new and more just society. I was even more surprised to find that the same social services being cut back by the wealthiest country in the world were being initiated and developed by one of the poorest: medical care, housing, a vast expansion of education for children and adults, nursery care for the children of working mothers, and so forth. And I realized that the secret lay in the capacity of the Nicaraguans to invent solutions in line with the limits of their resources and to inspire women and men, old and young, the poor and the rich to struggle for a cause worth their efforts. I wager that, in the United States as well, we will sooner or later discover that such inspiration and release of energy can come only as we are captivated by a similar vision and social project.

For many Latin Americans, *socialism* is no longer a word that bears threatening connotations. It is rather the term that serves best to identify the type of new economic and social order they are struggling to create. Sooner or later in a number of countries in Central and South America revolutionary regimes calling themselves socialist will come to power. As the product of the interaction of Christians and Marxists, they may well represent the beginning of a new stage in the historical development of socialism. They will not fit our stereotypes, and as long as we as a nation allow these stereotypes to distort our vision and determine our policy, the results will be disastrous for them and us.

The alternative open to us is, first of all, to understand what Latin Americans mean today when they speak of socialism. For most of those I know, this term means three things: (1) national economic independence so that the resources of each country can be used to meet the needs of its people according to goals determined by them; (2) an economic order the development of which responds to the needs of the vast majority of persons; and (3) a restructuring of power so that those now at the bottom can become participants in its use. I can see no reason why we in the United States should be upset by or opposed to these goals. Our major concern should be whether our policy contributes to or gets in the way of their achievement.

If we are able to make this shift in our attitude toward socialism in Latin America, we may discover something even more important: these developments in Latin America can help us to shape our vision of a more human future for ourselves. We will probably speak much more of *local self-reliance* than of socialism. But as we come to see more clearly the dead-end in which we are caught with the approaching end of the industrial era—with the energy crisis, the exhaustion of natural resources, the pollution of the natural environment, and the dehumanizing effects of large-scale bureaucratic organizations—our dreams may converge with theirs. We will set as our goal the creation of a social order in which women and men in local communities take upon themselves the responsibility to work together to meet an increasing number of their own needs and build networks of sharing and exchange with other such communities. In this way scarce resources can be used to sustain a more austere and yet richer life, a life enriched by a sense of economic security and well-being, a new experience of responsibility for and control over our existence, a discovery of new meaning in work and of new depth in human relationships.

This transformation has already begun. It is happening in some of our most depressed urban ghettoes as small groups of young blacks and Hispanics get together to build parks, grow vegetables on vacant lots once covered with debris, take over abandoned buildings and renovate them, and create small networks of mutual support. With a small amount of financial and technical help, they could go much further, organizing production cooperatives, small businesses, and neighborhood development projects. As people discover their capacity to meet their own needs and develop a new economic base, neighborhoods take on new life and hope is reborn. In like manner a wide variety of experiments making use of small-scale machinery and technologies for renewable energy development are going on in rural areas and small towns.

Thus far, all this is in its earliest stages and limited to small groups of people. Dreams are becoming reality; a new quality of life is being offered to us. As we in the United States choose this future for ourselves, we will no longer see the poor persons of the world as our enemies. Instead of competing with them for the diminishing natural resources of this planet, we will be engaged with them in a common struggle to use the riches of the earth to create conditions for a full life for all. In this way we may confirm Gandhi's belief that the "earth provides enough to satisfy every man's need, but not enough for every man's greed."

As we in the United States begin, once again, to dream of a "new heaven and a new earth," we will overcome our fear of communism and be able to relate more creatively to Marxian thought.

Many Latin American Christians have found that some Marxist categories of social analysis and perspectives on social transformation help them to understand what is happening in their countries and to work more effectively for change. And they can draw on Marxism in this way without becoming doctrinaire adherents to a total system. We can only stand to gain by being open to this same possibility. The shock of a new encounter with Marxism could help us go beyond the sterility of so much of our conservative and liberal thought and to create a new language of our own capable of broadening our horizons and producing more effective strategies for change. In this way, we would also provide a new generation with a greater depth of thought and a wider range of options, thus lessening the appeal of Marxism as a total system offering the only alternative to the status quo.

Twenty years ago Christians concerned about social justice were afraid of Marxism and its appeal to young people, especially those from Christian backgrounds. Marxists stood almost alone in the struggle for justice for the poor and in their willingness to pay the price of it. Today this has changed. Christians, partly as a result of their encounter with Marxism, are living out their commitment to the poor, have developed a rich body of social thought, and have demonstrated the power of biblical faith and Christian community to energize and orient the struggle of the dispossessed. More important still, in many places the Christians are the ones who are giving their lives in this cause.

Here too the Latin Americans may be pointing the way ahead for us. In a world that can survive only if it is transformed, Christians will live in fear of Marxism and of any other dynamic movement for change only as we continue to betray our faith. But when we learn to live it out—and, if necessary, to suffer for it—such fears will disappear. We will face difficult struggles within the movements we are a part of. We will always live in the tension between our vision of what could be and the reality of what is. But we will face these situations with a sense of confidence based on our rediscovery of the power of faith.

Chapter 8

Basic Christian Communities

In Latin America a new theology is finding expression in and giving shape to a new church. In the process of doing so, that theology is being enriched and transformed. The basic Christian communities, the grassroots nuclei of this emerging church of the poor, constitute the cornerstone of a new Reformation; at the same time, they are fast becoming a major political force.

These communities of faith are laying the foundation for a new type of democracy, in which common persons can be active participants; they are also making a major contribution toward the development of a mass movement for radical social change. In these small groups the poor find themselves in a milieu in which they feel at home, are affirmed as human beings, and discover their potential. The existence of the communities represents a major challenge not only to the established order but also to the policy of the U.S. government. As a result the poor persons in these communities are one of the groups being most violently persecuted by the regimes the United States supports. The existence and witness of the basic communities can become a resource for us as we seek, in the years ahead, to respond to the challenge of the poor persons of the world.

To give the reader some idea of what a base community is, I would like to describe the experience Nancy and I had when we visited one in Santiago, Chile. To get there we took the subway to the end of the line and then traveled by a bus to the point where it turned around. We found ourselves in the middle of a very poor neighborhood, in which the majority of heads of families had no steady, full-time jobs, due to the high rate of unemployment. People began to gather in a one-room shack they had built themselves, which was used not only for their religious meetings but for a wide range of community activities. When about thirty people had assembled, they began talking about their experiences of the past week: their frustration with not finding work anywhere, the fact that the city was cutting off the water of those unable to pay, personal and family problems of various members of the group, all this culminating with a number of stories of police harassment.

At this point a woman in the group stood up and said that she had found a biblical text she thought spoke to their discussion. With a great deal of difficulty—and helped by others—she read the words of St. Paul in 1 Corinthians about how God has chosen the weak to confound the strong and those who are "nobodies" to overthrow the existing order (1:27–28). Then a lively discussion began with many participating, including the priest and nun who were present. Several women spoke of how the community had given them a new sense of themselves and empowered them to speak and act. And then María, who had been an active member of the group since its beginning, told of her experience at the city market the previous Sunday. She was there selling a few items, as were hundreds of other jobless persons. Suddenly the police arrived, intending to arrest the men who were selling without a license and confiscate their goods. They began with a group near María. When they were about to haul them away, María decided she could not remain passive. With great fear, she stood up, placed herself between those men and the police, and declared: "If you're going to arrest them, you'll have to arrest me because I don't have a license either. Besides, you should be ashamed of yourselves, taking away from us the only chance we have to keep our children from starving." Gradually a number of other women nearby joined María, and the police walked away. When María finished her story, everybody applauded.

Bible study was followed by a time for planning for the week ahead, deciding who would take responsibility for things that needed to be done to help others in the community, the program of religious activities, and work on a number of specific projects.

This base community had initiated fourteen self-help projects in that *población*—for instance, soup kitchens, literacy classes, and child care—and for some of them they needed greater support than they were receiving. After these matters were settled, two new topics were raised for discussion: how to do something to stop the city from cutting off the water of those who could not pay their bills; and, whether or not the few who had regular jobs should run the risk of losing them by taking part in the demonstration being planned for the following Sunday by the base communities as a protest against unemployment. They all wanted to be part of this movement even though it might lead to beatings and arrests, but those who were employed needed the help of the community to decide where their responsibility lay.

The meeting ended with a time of prayer. As we mingled among the members and then walked toward the bus, we realized that we had witnessed a miracle. The rejects of society had discovered their own worth; people formerly isolated and abandoned had begun to share almost everything with each other. Together they were taking unusual initiatives in local self-reliance and were beginning to realize that they had power to bring about changes in their situation. And they had more vitality and energy and greater hope for the future than we had found anywhere else in Chile during our weeks there. A priest and a nun had lived among these people for a number of years, had communicated a vision to them, and had worked with them to empower them—and their efforts had borne fruit.

Latin Americans associated with these communities claim, quite rightfully I believe, that what they have developed is a new church. As has happened frequently in the past in situations in which the church has become acculturated, lost its vitality, and seemed to be dying, unexpected new life has appeared. It has broken out when small groups of women and men, agonizing over the state of their lives and the world, have found in the gospel a compelling message, which up to that time had been largely hidden. In this instance it is the discovery of what the kingdom of God represents for the poor of the earth. Its coming has been announced to them. Starting from them and in their midst, God builds this new order in history. Consequently, the church of Jesus Christ is made up of those who are rejected, despised, and abandoned—those who are considered useless, incapable of doing anything, and have believed what society says about them. In the church the poor meet and discover that they can think and act, that they have rights and a special vocation. As one theologian has put it, "The church is the means by which the poor enter History."

In this church of the poor, several elements combine to make it what it is and determine how it functions.

THE POOR AND THE BIBLE

The basic Christian communities are essentially *religious* communities in which the religious world of the poor is honored and transformed as they read and study the Bible together. In the words of Cardinal Arns, Archbishop of São Paulo,

> People do not come to the BCCs [basic Christian communities] when there is no praying or singing. They may come four or five times to organize practical things, but nothing further will come of it. When, however, people pray and sing, when they feel themselves together, when the Gospel is read and, on this basis, concrete actions are organized and the national situation is analyzed, then the groups remain united. Along with the Gospels, this religiosity is the most valuable element in the BCCs.

Priests and theologians no longer look down on the "primitive" religion of the poor or try to replace it with "correct" theological concepts. They now realize that this religion touches the core of the poor's existence and can become a powerful resource for transformation. Orthodox theological language may mean very little to poor peasants, but the Bible speaks to them directly. Its stories connect with their story, as does much of its imagery and symbolic language.

Over the last hundred years, Protestants have taken the initiative in putting the Bible in the hands of the people. But now the basic Christian communities are going far beyond the Protestants in carrying forward the revolution they started. When people in base communities read the Bible together, they find that *it relates to all aspects of their life in the world. It describes their struggle in society and helps them articulate their hopes for a more human and just order.* Not having been taught to separate the spiritual and the material, the individual and the social, they find in the Bible "one single Word for one single world."

We Protestants gave the Bible to the people and then too often proceeded to tell them what it said. The basic Christian communities function on the assumption that the Holy Spirit will lead the poor to understand the Word as they share their insights with each other. Biblical experts and those with more biblical and theological training may be present, as participants in the discussion. But their knowledge is just one of the elements that contribute to the process of learning. The result is often a richness and depth of understanding that surprises and humbles the experts. The poor realize that they can think for themselves and *discover* the truth rather than *receive* it as it is handed down to them by others. In this way those who have been silent begin to speak with their own voice.

Born-again Christians speak in glowing terms of being saved. They have undergone a profound experience of transformation in which the power of sin in their lives has been broken and they have found peace and joy. Many members of base communities speak in similar terms of what has happened to them—with one difference. Their experience of new life is closely linked to their day-to-day struggle against oppression, as they come to value themselves as persons, learn to share with and help each other in community, risk their lives in a common struggle for justice, and look to the future with hope.

A NEW FORM OF COMMUNITY

In basic Christian communities the poor are creating a *new quality of life in community.* People who live in the same neighborhood, often on the same street or within a few blocks of each other, get together frequently in small groups. They may assemble in the home of one of the members or in a one-room community center they have built to serve the entire neighborhood. In some cases a priest or a nun is present and most likely lives there and shares their daily struggle. In this community the poor feel completely at home. Their language and culture are affirmed and respected. It is their world.

Traditionally, in the rural areas and small cities, the poor have survived in part because of the tight kinship networks they maintained. Whenever an individual or family was in desperate need, they could count on other members of the wider family to help see them through. With the movement of population and the social changes that have come about in recent decades, much of this has been lost and nuclear family units often find themselves totally alone in the large cities or even in rural areas.

In the base communities the poor themselves are re-creating these support networks. The spirit of family solidarity, which led them to share the little bit of food they had or their cramped living quarters with other members, has now re-emerged. It finds expression in a new family of faith. A new richness of spiritual life provides new motivation for this and leads to a stronger sense of unity and solidarity. Once again, the sharing of possessions described in the Book of Acts (2:42–47; 4:32–37) is the natural outgrowth of a new pentecost. In São Paulo, during a recent strike, the families of the strikers that still had something to eat decided to contribute one tablespoon of rice each day to help those who were completely destitute.

But the most revolutionary thing that is happening in these circles is the radical change that is occurring in the way the poor look at themselves and their world. As they read the Gospel and discuss it and pray together, they come to think of themselves as persons of worth. They develop a new sense of self-confidence as they realize that they can speak their own word and act together to change their situation. The power of the gospel working in the life of the community breaks the grip of internalized oppression, which led them to believe that they were inferior beings and thus kept them down. Frantz Fanon, working among the peasants in Algeria, came to the conclusion that this weight of oppression had so destroyed the spirit of the peasants that they would be able to liberate themselves from it only after they had killed a settler. The basic Christian communities offer an alternative. Those who participate in them are finding that oppressive power has been broken. And as this burden is lifted from them, the fires of hope are kindled and they show amazing courage even in the face of violent repression.

What is happening here is that a new form of social organization is in the process of creation, and as this happens, the poor are winning for themselves an authentic place in society for the first time in history. More than this, the poor themselves are creating a model for future society. When they sit around a circle in the base communities, they are expressing visibly their break with hierarchical—or bureaucratic—organization. The crucial thing is mutual empowerment, and those who are recognized as having special gifts are expected to use them to *facilitate* more responsible participation on the part of all members. The foundation is laid for the exercise of power *from the bottom up,* in the wider society as well as in the church.

A NEW REFORMATION

Once again a movement of reformation within the church is laying the foundation for a new social order. In the base communities the poor are not only giving shape to it on a small scale but also are being trained to take the lead in bringing it into existence in other areas of society.

Here again, Roman Catholics have revived one of the major emphases of the Protestant Reformation of the sixteenth century and are now putting it into practice in a way that Protestants have never been able to do. The idea of the priesthood of all believers and the vocation of all Christians to use their particular gifts for upbuilding the church as the body of Christ is being taken seriously, not just given lip service. If the base community is functioning properly, all members are being raised up to a position of importance and given an opportunity to speak their word and use their unique talents to serve the community. For the efficient functioning of the group, specific ministries are recognized. Certain people must take responsibility for the liturgy, the educational program, the organization of care for the sick and the most needy, the coordination of specific projects, and so forth. But women and men are chosen for these tasks by the whole community and for a limited period of time. A few natural leaders in each group are identified and given opportunities for further training, but they are encouraged to serve the community and not use their extra training as a means of dominating others. Persons from outside the community—a priest, a nun, a pastoral agent—may play an important role in organizing and helping these communities. But here again their role is radically different from that of the traditional priest. The pastoral agents, who are coming more and more to the fore, represent a new vocation within the church. They are not oriented toward having an ecclesiastical career or exercising power. Usually they volunteer their services or receive only enough for subsistence, and they live among the people they serve. Especially in situations of political repression, they find that their situation is financially, socially, and politically as vulnerable as that of anyone else.

In Brazil, where the basic Christian communities have grown most rapidly, steps are now being taken to reorganize certain dioceses so that those below can play a major role in the decision-making process within the structure of the diocese itself. In São Paulo, for example, Archbishop Arns has taken the lead in developing a pattern by which the base communities decide upon the priorities they want to propose for the diocese and make them known through a process of discussion and decision making within a new structure of representation. The goals of the diocese for each triennium are determined in a convention in which the representatives of the base communities participate with bishops and priests.

A POLITICAL FORCE

This vital religious movement is fast becoming *the most powerful political force working for change in Latin America*—often to the surprise of its own members. As they discover that the Gospel is good news for all aspects of life and that Jesus Christ is present in their struggle for liberation, their newly discovered strength, their vision, and their passion must inevitably express themselves politically.

They soon find themselves involved in creating a new social order locally, at the grassroots, and thus participating in a new experiment in popular democracy. In his study of Brazilian basic Christian communities, Alvaro Barreiro states it this way:

> It is at the grassroots that new systems are tried out. A beginning is made by working together on property held in

common, giving one another help in building dwellings, cultivating the fields and group-buying of food products. This practice finally leads to self-administration by grassroots groups, which are thus seen as a means of reacting against centralization of power and the bureaucracy of the technocrats [Barreiro 1982].

As the poor begin to understand what the old, established order is doing to them, form cooperatives, and take small actions to bring about change, they are seen by the ruling oligarchies as a great threat, which must be eliminated at all costs. And when soldiers, police, or paramilitary groups massacre entire families and villages, the members of the base communities are forced to the conclusion that their real enemy is the established regime. At the same time they realize that those who are risking their lives in the struggle for justice—whether Marxists or others—are on their side. Often they decide to join the rebel cause, seeing in it their only chance of survival as well as the opportunity to establish the new society already existing in embryo in their midst.

Charles Clements, the Quaker and doctor from North America who recently spent a year practicing medicine in one of the rebel zones of El Salvador, tells of his conversation with a pregnant peasant woman who told him that seven of her children had died when the soldiers came to her village and blew up a house in which thirty-four women and children were gathered. When he asked her why they had not tried to hide from the soldiers, she replied: "That was *before* we knew that the army was the enemy."

This shift in perception on the part of the poor has introduced several new factors in the revolutionary struggle in Central America. Members of the base communities are now playing a major role in it. The claim that the rebels are Marxist-Leninists is a gross error of fact. Christians and Marxists are working together in this struggle, and the broad base of it in many places is primarily Christian. It is constituted by persons who have discovered their own worth and power, who are determined to participate fully in the exercise of power after the revolution succeeds, and who will fight to preserve their own grassroots religious and social organizations. And as has already happened in Nicaragua, this presence of the base communities gives reason for hope that the new revolutionary societies will be quite different from what now exists in Cuba or in other Third World socialist states.

Moreover, the development of the base communities is having an important influence on Marxists as well. During a recent visit to Chile, I met on two occasions with groups of men and women who had been active in the Allende regime, some of them in rather important positions. When they found out that I had been in contact with basic Christian communities in various countries, our discussion focused on what was happening in them. These people spoke a great deal about their concern for the poor and their efforts to do something for them. But they confessed that their attitude had been too elitist. They had thought they had had the correct analysis of society and could pass it on to the poor. They realized, however, that they had not been concerned enough to create space *for the poor* in the new society, to empower them, or to set up political structures in which the poor would effectively exercise power. And they admitted that their perspective had changed because of what they had learned about the base communities and through their contact with the work of Catholics in the popular church. They were especially anxious to study this movement and learn from it. I have since discovered that elsewhere in Latin America this same attitude exists in other such groups.

A NEXT STEP FOR US?

For those of us concerned about the state of the church today, this "church that is born among the poor" may have much to say to us. What we have here is the *resurrection* of the church. The old church had to die, and men and women had to die to it. Out of that death, new life and new communities have appeared, the shape of which could not have been imagined by those still in bondage to the old institution. The new church has emerged among the poor, as it did in the beginning. They are the ones who have understood what the Gospel is really about, grasped its simplicity, and humbly lived out the faith, hope, and love of which it speaks. Faith has emerged from impotence. And what has happened in Latin America can happen elsewhere if we are willing to follow the same path, by turning toward the poor and allowing them to transform us.

As word spreads about the church of the poor in Latin America, I find a great deal of interest in the United States in base communities as a new model for the church, especially in urban areas. And Latin Americans, who think of the church in North America as having great wealth and power yet being unable to change national policies, often wonder why we cannot follow their example.

Charles Clements tells of a conversation a group of peasants had with him before he left El Salvador. On the basis of news reports they had heard about the Reagan administration and what it was doing, one of them remarked: "So many people are opposed to Reagan's policies and are suffering because of them. Blacks, Hispanics, old people, everybody who's poor. A big majority is opposed to what their government is doing in Central America. They're against the arms race and they're afraid of nuclear war. Then why don't they do something about it? Why are they so powerless? We ought to show them how to organize basic Christian communities."

This man may have a point. But the experience of the base communities can be of help to us in the First World only if we realize what they represent. If we look to them to find a method, a model or technique that we can simply duplicate in North America, we are wasting our time. If we liken them to Bible study groups or "house churches," which were popular in some circles not long ago, we will never grasp what they really are.

The power of the base communities lies in the fact that the poor—with some help from others, to be sure—have been grasped and transformed by good news from the Bible, by an offer of new life and a message of liberation most of us have not yet heard. In their extreme poverty and total insecurity, they have been enabled to share everything and experience the presence and power of the Holy Spirit, as did the earliest Christians. And their passion for liberation and their solidarity with each other have become such a subversive force that they are being persecuted, tortured, and killed. If we want to take up the challenge of the basic Christian communities, the question we have to ask ourselves is this: What would it mean for us here to follow a similar process in North America?

The whole thing began in Latin America when a number of Christians from the middle and upper classes decided to live and work with the poor, become part of a community of faith made up primarily of the dispossessed, and find a way to support their struggle. Originally they saw this as a necessary step toward the formation of a new church and new social movements which would be *of* the poor and which the poor would lead. But along the way, they discovered something else: in this sharing with the poor, those who were not poor were enabled to understand what was happening in their society. They perceived dimensions of the Gospel they had never seen before and experienced a richness of life in community they had not previously known.

In our case, I think we have no choice but to do something similar. We are so much at home in the values and lifestyle of the dominant order that nothing short of the closest contact with the suffering of those being destroyed by it will shock us into a new awareness of how our society works or open our eyes to what the Gospel says about it. We are so individualistic and so obsessed with getting and keeping all we can that only the willingness of the poorest to share the little bit they have and support each other can show us what Christian community is all about. It is when we stand with the rejects and support their cause that we can grasp the meaning of love and justice.

How we go about this movement toward the poor is a question for which there is no simple answer. We have before us a variety of options to be explored. Nuns from many different orders are following the example of their Latin American sisters. In the United States those who are now living and working with the poor have formed a national association for mutual support and to learn from each other. In Protestant circles, the Sojourners Community in Washington has pioneered in establishing small households, largely of young men and women, which are in the ghettoes and have similar objectives to the Latin American base communities. In both Catholic and Protestant circles, many initiatives of this sort are being taken. What is distinctive about these developments is the commitment of their members to *solidarity* rather than charity. The former paternalistic attitude of "do-gooders" has been replaced by the desire to join with the poor in their struggle for a just cause, learn from them, and thus be prepared to work more effectively among middle-class Christians.

Short of these more dramatic moves that most of us are probably not yet prepared to make, there are innumerable opportunities for us to learn from and develop new relationships with those who are victims of our present system. While teaching at Princeton Seminary, I frequently held seminars in which blacks and Third World students were in the majority. I soon realized that most white students had never been confronted by the witness of the oppressed peoples of the world. When it happened, they were shocked and offended. Some of them were also transformed. They developed new relationships, and began to see previously unimagined opportunities to work with others for the cause of social justice.

A few women and men in any local church can take the initiative in bringing together a small group for dialogue, study, and action along these same lines. In the United States there are large numbers of blacks and Hispanics in many of our communities, and in all First World nations there are often students and other visitors from Third World countries. They are eager for contact and relationships with us and complain that they have few opportunities to talk with us about things which most concern them. At the same time, the number of impoverished people in our local neighborhoods is increasing from year to year. Among the elderly persons in our churches, we may discover those whose lives are being diminished and destroyed by an unjust system. If we do not undertake new ventures of this sort, it is only our own indifference that keeps us from doing so.

Another possible approach here is for us to become a community as we help each other understand and deal with *our own oppression*. In this advanced technological society, those of us who are more privileged are also victims. If we are willing to explore what this means with some seriousness, we will discover that we also are compelled to struggle against a system of domination and exploitation and realize that the dispossessed are our allies in this long-term struggle.

A few months ago Nancy and I were invited to work with members of a local church in just such an exploration. We found a group of twenty men and women who were keenly interested in this project and were willing to dedicate six consecutive Sunday evenings to it. The first session was an exciting one, as all the members of the group identified one or more areas in which they felt oppressed: self-oppression caused by internalizing current values, problems in male-female relationships, oppressive work situations, the sense of political powerlessness when trying to work for changes in society, and so forth. But when we tried to work on these specific issues, problems arose. Those most aware of their oppression were often afraid to explore it in depth. Many members of the group had never thought about the relation between their own experience of oppression and the overall social and economic system. Even when this was brought to their attention, they had no conceptual tools with which to work on it. And although those present had been active church members for some time, they saw little or no connection between their religious faith and the issues they were facing. Their faith was not a resource either for understanding or action. At the last session some members of the group expressed frustration because they had not been able to make more progress, but all were convinced that the experience had been a valuable one for them.

Our own conclusion was that for white, middle-class persons in the First World, dealing with their own oppression will be a long and painful process. It can be productive to the degree that it is undertaken in community by women and men who know they can no longer avoid facing it. In Latin America this process was greatly accelerated when repressive regimes began to persecute groups in which such awareness was growing. It may well be that something similar will happen in the First World—and much sooner than we now expect. If that possibility exists, then the sooner groups of Christians get together to study what is happening around them and respond to it, the better prepared we will be to meet this challenge in time.

If we come to realize that community, in the Christian sense, means a rich sharing of life with each other and with the oppressed as we struggle together for a new and more just society, then *the most important thing we can do at the present time to contribute to that struggle is to give shape to and participate in this type of community*. Ideologies, strategies for action, and political movements are all necessary, and there are many people who will give primary attention to them. But if Christians have a specific responsibility and opportunity at this moment, it is to form small groups in which people can engage in serious study and action while exploring the resources of their faith and learning how to keep each other going in a long and difficult struggle.

This, I believe, is the most valuable lesson we can learn from the basic Christian communities in Latin America. They have succeeded in creating a milieu in which persons have grown rapidly in their understanding of their society as well as in their commitment to change it. The communities themselves are giving shape to a new vision of society and preparing many men and women to insert themselves in the political struggle and play a major role in it. In São Paulo, for example, they have provided a new base and orientation for the labor movement and have led to the formation of a new labor party that is organized in such a way as to offer the urban poor their first real opportunity to participate in the exercise of power.

I believe that in the First World groups working for peace have already begun moving toward this type of community. As their early efforts have been rejected by those in power, they have felt frustrated and at the same time have come to understand better the nature of the problem with which they are dealing. A greater sense of urgency is accompanied by the desire to be better informed and to understand why our society functions the way it does. The compulsion to do something before it is too late is matched by the recognition that the normal political process is not capable of meeting this challenge. These groups will be able to continue only if their members discover how to relate to each other at a much deeper level, engage in careful social analysis, and explore anew the resources offered by their heritage of faith.

The formation of such communities will not be easy. Many attempts will end up in failure; a relatively long period of trial and error may be necessary before successes are realized. But the Latin American experience shows us that those who are committed to the struggle for life in the midst of sclerosis and death can hope for breakthroughs to occur, perhaps when they least expect them. We can also trust that we will find new resources for living from our faith and from each other and that our hope for the future will be strengthened when our efforts are least successful. We may eventually also realize that we are beginning to live a new quality of life and may be participating in experiments that could produce new forms of economic, political, and social organization.

In line with what I have been saying in these pages, the real test of our response to the challenge of the basic Christian communities will be our willingness to shape our communities around identification with the poor in their struggle for justice. Our perception of what is happening in the United States and in the rest of the First World and our actions even for the cause of peace will be superficial until we experience directly what is happening to the dispossessed and determine to find out why this injustice is built into our system. If we dare to take those steps, then we will also see how badly we need to be part of a small community of faith. I cannot point to any groups I know of that are now doing this. But we do not have to have a blueprint in order to begin. We know we can cross racial and class barriers and find those who are willing to explore joint efforts with us. We know how to go about analyzing our society with the help of those who are its victims. And in some of the poorest urban and rural areas, there are already a rather large number of ventures in local self-reliance that may be pointing the way to the future—and in which we might participate. As that happens, we will be in a position to learn from each other and develop strategies for more effective political action.

THE PROCESS OF LIBERATION IN LATIN AMERICA

As I have traveled in Central and South America in recent years, I have been especially impressed by one fact: The men and women among whom I have moved, especially in Christian circles, have the sense that they are entering a new era in history; they are engaged in constructing a new social order offering, for the first time, life and hope to the masses of poor persons. Their thoughts as well as their lives express the excitement that goes with participation in such an enterprise.

This is the milieu in which the theology of liberation has developed. It has made a major contribution to the articulation of this vision and has helped sustain the struggle of those motivated by it. At the same time this theology has been shaped by and is continually being reworked in the midst of this struggle.

The ultimate challenge the theologians of liberation lay before us is this: Can we, in dialogue with them, begin to perceive and respond to our situation in a similar way? This, in my judgment, is much more important than whether we agree with their approach or appropriate their system of thought.

If we concern ourselves with the question, By what process did they arrive at this point?, several things stand out.

1. Early on, a few women and men were so overwhelmed by the oppression and suffering around them that they could no longer continue living their lives as they had. They felt compelled to identify with the poor, take their suffering upon themselves, and join in their struggle for liberation. This led them into a new engagement with their religious heritage. Often to their surprise, they found that heritage could reinterpret what was happening around them and provide them with resources for a new quality of life.

2. In the midst of this involvement, they began to perceive the contours of a new world worth living and dying for. In it, the dispossessed, deprived, and displaced men and women of the *Third* World will have a chance to fulfil their potential. A social system in which an elite few enjoy great wealth at the expense of the many, and take pleasure in exercising power over those they render powerless, is giving way to this new order. Men and women are learning to work together to produce what they need and share the little they have. They are discovering how to raise up and empower each other and thus create a new space for human fulfillment. In the basic Christian communities they experience the first fruits of the new age. At the same time some of those who are in a privileged position are realizing that this social transformation offers new life to them as well.

3. As this utopian vision begins to take shape in a community of faith and in the wider society, the response of the rich and powerful is to rely more and more on repression, torture, and assassination to preserve what they have. Their attacks upon Christians have been especially vicious. But thus far this persecution has served to expose the evils of the established order and strengthen the resolve of those struggling to change it.

THE PROCESS OF LIBERATION IN THE FIRST WORLD

My hope for the future of the United States and the rest of the First World is based on my belief that we can and will follow a similar process in response to our situation.

1. We too are surrounded by tremendous injustice and suffering, enough to disturb our consciences and raise questions about our self-centered lives and careers. For many of us, our first awareness of this has come from living or traveling in Third World countries. But that experience helps to open our eyes to what is happening immediately around us: the despair of those, in our affluent society, who are deprived of decent food, shelter, and medical care and the broken lives of the unemployed, the elderly, those discriminated against for reasons of race or sex, and those dehumanized by our technological and bureaucratic society.

In Latin America the religious orders made it possible for hundreds if not thousands of their members to live with the dispossessed and take up their cause. Most of us do not belong to such orders. That only underlines the importance of experimenting with the formation of new communities capable of performing this task. If and when that happens, we too may discover that our religious heritage will once again come alive, renewing our vision and releasing our energies.

2. In a society deeply troubled because it can dream of no future beyond the continuation of what it is now—and is in danger of losing—the vision of the people of the Third World can offer us a new future as well. The bankruptcy of a technocratic society, which has destroyed human initiative, encouraged superficial interpersonal relationships, and diminished human worth, opens the way for us to imagine and begin to create a more human society for ourselves. Here the oppressed people of the world are pointing the way. They challenge the poor and marginalized in our countries to create grassroots social, economic, and political structures responsive to their needs and to learn how to share with and empower each other. Small steps in this direction could lay the foundation for a new historical era for the peoples of the First World as well—even those of us who assume that we have most to lose from any radical change.

3. As groups of Christians in the First World succeed in articulating and living such a vision, they can expect to face increasing hostility and persecution from those in positions of power. The crisis of our system of values and our institutions leads those most threatened by it to be fearful and do everything in their power to

conceal the real situation and destroy those movements trying to bring about radical change. When significant numbers of women and men come alive as they struggle for social transformation, their witness may well be met by increasing repression.

This is nothing new in Christian history. When it happens, small communities of faith find the resources not only to resist but to grow stronger. This is now evident throughout Latin America; sooner or later we will see it in our countries as well.

If there is one major difference between Latin American Christians and us, it is this: they have already lived out much of what is still ahead of us. In doing so they have produced the theology of liberation and created the base communities. Their thought and experience are now available as gifts to us. They are ours, to be drawn upon as we respond to the challenges before us.

Works Cited

Barreiro, Alvaro. 1982. *Basic Ecclesial Communities: The Evangelization of the Poor.* Trans. Barbara Campbell. Maryknoll, N.Y.: Orbis Books.

Bloch, Ernst. 1972. *Atheism and Christianity: The Religion of the Exodus and the Kingdom.* Trans. J. T. Swann. New York: Herder and Herder.

Bonhoeffer, Dietrich. 1978. *Letters and Papers from Prison.* Enl. ed. New York: Macmillan Co.

Cochrane, Charles Norris. 1940. *Christianity and Classical Culture: A Study of Thought and Action from Augustus to Augustine.* New York: Oxford University Press.

Croatto, J. Severino. 1981. *Exodus: A Hermeneutics of Freedom.* Trans. Salvator Attanasio. Maryknoll, N.Y.: Orbis Books.

Cussiánovich, Alejandro. 1979. *Religious Life and the Poor: Liberation Theology Perspectives.* Trans. John Drury. Maryknoll, N.Y.: Orbis Books.

Dussel, Enrique D. 1978. *Ethics and the Theology of Liberation.* Trans. Bernard F. McWilliams. Maryknoll, N.Y.: Orbis Books.

Elizondo, Virgilio. 1983. *Galilean Journey: The Mexican-American Promise.* Maryknoll, N.Y.: Orbis Books.

Ellacuría, Ignacio. 1976. *Freedom Made Flesh: The Mission of Christ and His Church.* Trans. John Drury. Maryknoll, N.Y.: Orbis Books.

Gilder, George. 1981. *Wealth and Poverty.* New York: Basic Books.

Gottwald, Norman K. 1979. *The Tribes of Yahweh: A Sociology of Liberated Israel, 1250–1050 B.C.E.* Maryknoll, N.Y.: Orbis Books.

Gutiérrez, Gustavo. 1973. *A Theology of Liberation: History, Politics and Salvation.* Trans. and ed. Sister Caridad Inda and John Eagleson. Maryknoll, N.Y.: Orbis Books.

Jeremias, Joachim. 1981. *New Testament Theology: The Proclamation of Jesus.* Trans. John Bowden. New York: Charles Scribner's Sons.

Lesbaupin, Ivo. 1977. "The Latin American Bishop and Socialism," in *Christianity and Socialism*, ed. J. B. Metz and J. P. Jossua. Concilium 105. New York: The Seabury Press.

Miranda, José Porfirio. 1977. *Being and the Messiah: The Message of St. John.* Trans. John Eagleson. Maryknoll, N.Y.: Orbis Books.

————. 1974. *Marx and the Bible: A Critique of the Philosophy of Oppression.* Trans. John Eagleson. Maryknoll, N.Y.: Orbis Books.

Napier, B. Davie. 1981. *Song of the Vineyard: A Guide through the Old Testament.* Rev. ed. Philadelphia: Fortress Press.

Piven, Frances Fox, and Richard A. Cloward. 1982. *The New Class War: Reagan's Attack on the Welfare State and Its Consequences.* New York: Pantheon Books.

Rad, Gerhard von. 1965. *Old Testament Theology.* Vol. 2., *The Theology of Israel's Prophetic Traditions.* Trans. D. M. G. Stalker. New York: Harper and Row.

Rosenstock-Huessy, Eugen. 1969. *Out of Revolution: Autobiography of Western Man.* Norwich, Vt.: Argo Books.

Silva Gotay, Samuel. 1981. *El pensamiento cristiano revolucionario en América Latina y el Caribe.* Salamanca, Spain: Sígueme.

Wolff, Hans Walter. 1981. *Micah the Prophet.* Trans. Ralph D. Gehrke. Philadelphia: Fortress Press.

Other Orbis Books . . .

WE DRINK FROM OUR OWN WELLS
The Spiritual Journey of a People
by Gustavo Gutiérrez
Preface by Henri Nouwen
"The publication of this book is an extremely significant event in the development of liberation theology. It is the fulfillment of a promise that was implicit in Gutiérrez's *A Theology of Liberation* which appeared in 1971 and soon became the charter for many Latin American theologians and pastoral workers. Gutiérrez realized from the beginning that a theology which is not coming forth from an authentic encounter with the Lord can never be fruitful. It took more than ten years before he had the occasion to fully develop this spirituality, but it was worth waiting for."
Henri J. M. Nouwen

"Gutiérrez has introduced a new spirituality, viz., the spirituality of solidarity with the poor."   *Edward Schillebeeckx*

ISBN 0-88344-707-X   *176pp. Paper $7.95*

BLACK AND REFORMED
Apartheid, Liberation, and the Calvinist Tradition
by Allan Boesak
"In this collection, Allan Boesak continues to raise for those of us outside South Africa the issue of liberation of all people in that country. He creatively relates the black struggle for freedom in South Africa to the liberating message of Jesus Christ without sacrificing the universal note of the gospel."   *James H. Cone,*
Union Theological Seminary, New York

ISBN 0-88344-148-9   *192pp. Paper $8.95*

CHRIST IN A PONCHO
Witnesses to the Nonviolent Struggles in Latin America
by Adolfo Pérez Esquivel
Winner of the 1980 Nobel Peace Prize
"A source book on the struggles of the oppressed of Latin America. Along with the moving testimony of this devout Christian layman to

peace, nonviolence, and justice, we read the words of the mothers of Argentina, the manifestoes of striking workers, and the pastorals of bishops. This makes for excellent primary source material." *Sojourners*

ISBN 0-88344-104-7 *139pp. Paper $6.95*

FOLLOWING CHRIST IN A CONSUMER SOCIETY
The Spirituality of Cultural Resistance
by John Francis Kavanaugh

"Kavanaugh succeeds in combining a sharp and uncompromising analysis of our contemporary consumer culture with gentle, compassionate and hope-filled reflection on the power of the Gospel to transform our cluttered lives. For the social activists who have lost confidence in the spiritual wellsprings of their activism, and for those who do not see the connections between their religious faith and economic and political issues, the author offers new confidence in inescapable connections."

Alternatives

ISBN 0-88344-090-3 *186pp. Paper $6.95*

THE RELIGIOUS ROOTS OF REBELLION
Christians in Central American Revolutions
by Phillip Berryman

"Phillip Berryman by training, experience, and commitment is uniquely equipped to interpret the dominant role of Christians in the ongoing Central American revolutions. From my longtime knowledge of him, of his works, and his writings, I had anticipated an important book. What he has written far outstrips my expectations, a systematic analysis resting on a bedrock of factual record.

"The liberating role is new for the church in Central America. Here in the United States we are deluged with lies and distortions concerning this role which has become central in the struggle of the people of the region for justice and dignity. Berryman's book could not have come at a more timely moment. We are all indebted to him for the convincing and thoroughly documented evaluation of a church that is being born in suffering in Central America, a church that offers hope to all of us. This is the authoritative statement against which all other accounts will be judged."

Gary MacEoin

"This is a provocative and important contribution to understanding the role of Catholicism in the struggle for justice in Central America. Phillip Berryman writes with the sensitivity and passion of a Christian who has lived the biblical option for the poor." *Penny Lernoux*

ISBN 0-88344-105-5 *464pp. Paper $19.95*

HOPING AGAINST ALL HOPE
by Dom Helder Camara
Powerful prose and poetry from the Brazilian archbishop internationally known for his advocacy of the poor and oppressed.

"Dom Helder is living daily with one of the most excruciating problems of our time: What are the grounds for hope for those who are powerless and know only one defeat after another? There are no clear rational answers to these questions today that make much sense to us, but there are a few people around the world who keep going—and help keep others going—hoping against hope. Dom Helder is one of these."

Richard Shaull

ISBN 0-88344-192-6 *illus., 96pp. Paper $4.95*

MYSTIC OF LIBERATION
A Portrait of Bishop Pedro Casaldáliga of Brazil
by Teófilo Cabestrero
"An inspiring account of one man's struggle against institutionalized oppression and greed in the backlands of Brazil. His defense of the rights of the Indians and small farmers living in the area has brought him into frequent conflict with Brazilian land companies, multinational corporations operating in the Amazon territory, and unfriendly civil authorities. On more than one occasion he has been the target of hired assassins. This book records his reflections on his priestly ministry, on the injustices his people suffer, on the evils of capitalism, and on the state of the Catholic Church in Brazil. The result is a striking portrait of a charismatic man of God and of the people and the church he serves so unselfishly." *Choice*

ISBN 0-88344-324-4 *illus., 224pp. Paper $7.95*

BIBLE OF THE OPPRESSED
by Elsa Tamez
"Elsa Tamez leads us through a systematic study of the words for oppression in the Bible. The theme of oppression and liberation is seen as the substance within history through which divine revelation unfolds. This is a careful and critical study in biblical theology. Tamez has written a biblical study that is both scholarly and usable for lay Bible study groups."

Sojourners

"For those of us eager to hear the voices of Latin American women, this book is doubly welcome! Writing from a perspective of those oppressed by poverty and sexism, Elsa Tamez has brought us a wealth of analysis of the biblical understanding of oppression." *Letty M. Russell, Yale Univ.*

ISBN 0-88344-035-0 *80pp. Paper $5.95*

THE BEATITUDES
To Evangelize as Jesus Did
by Segundo Galilea
An inspirational treatment of the Beatitudes of both Luke and Matthew by a popular writer of spirituality.

"Long experience in pastoral activity has qualified Galilea, one of Latin America's best-known theologians, to direct others on the way to spiritual maturity. His message is written in a style that makes sense to anyone, lay or expert, ready to give assent to the radical challenge of the Gospel."
Spirituality Today

"The warmth and openness with which Galilea preaches this gospel should inspire the activist to prayer, the pious to action, and all of us to a deeper reliance on the roots of our faith."
Sojourners

ISBN 0-88344-344-9 *128pp. Paper $5.95*

MINISTERS OF GOD, MINISTERS OF THE PEOPLE
Testimonies of Faith from Nicaragua
by Teófilo Cabestrero
Extensive interviews with Ernesto Cardenal, Minister of Culture, Fernando Cardenal, Youth Movement Coordinator, and Miguel d'Escoto, Foreign Minister.

"The focus of these conversations is on the men's perceptions of the connections between their religious vocation and their government functions; each sees his government responsibilities as a means of expressing Christian love for his people in practical service. The statements resonate with deeply felt conviction. Highly recommended for public, church, and academic libraries seeking a balanced view of Nicaragua today."
Library Journal

ISBN 0-88344-335-X *160pp. Paper $6.95*

THE GOSPEL IN SOLENTINAME
(four volumes)
by Ernesto Cardenal
"Farmers and fishermen in a remote village in Nicaragua join their priest for dialogues on Bible verses. Here is a translation (earthy epithets intact) of the tape-recorded conversations. Highly recommended to confront the complacent with the stark realities of religious and political consciousness in the Third World."
Library Journal

"Upon reading this book, I want to do so many things—burn all my other books which at best seem like hay, soggy with mildew. I now know who (not what) is the church and how to celebrate church in the Eucharist. The dialogues are intense, profound, radical. *The Gospel in Solentiname* calls us home." *Carroll Stuhlmueller*

ISBN 0-88344-176-4   *Vol. 1, 288pp. $8.95*
ISBN 0-88344-175-6   *Vol. 2, 272pp. $8.95*
ISBN 0-88344-174-8   *Vol. 3, 320pp. $8.95*
ISBN 0-88344-173-X   *Vol. 4, 288pp. $8.95*
                               (all volumes paperback)

THE GOSPEL IN ART BY THE PEASANTS OF SOLENTINAME
edited by Philip & Sally Scharper

Thirty-one stunning, full-color prints of Nicaraguan peasants' depictions of the gospel stories. The texts facing each painting are commentaries of the peasants on the Gospel passage relating to that painting. No other time or place offers us such a detailed and comprehensive record of what "ordinary" Christians made of the Gospel in the context of their own lives."

ISBN 0-88344-382-1   *70pp. Cloth $9.95*

BASIC ECCLESIAL COMMUNITIES
The Evangelization of the Poor
by Alvaro Barreiro

"Inspired by his experience with the basic ecclesial communities of Brazil, Alvaro Barreiro has written a simple yet succinct synthesis of the biblical foundations for the evangelical option of the poor as manifested in this movement. These communities are shown to be truly the church itself at its basic level, seeking 'to rediscover what is most central to Christianity and to put the Church back into the life that is lived daily again.' " *International Bulletin of Missionary Research*

"This book offers one of the few sources of solid information on base communities in English." *Today's Parish*

ISBN 0-88344-026-1   *96pp. Paper $5.95*

ARCHBISHOP ROMERO
Martyr of Salvador
by Plácido Erdozaín
Foreword by Jorge Lara-Braud

"Follows the political development of murdered Salvadoran Archbishop Oscar Romero. Written in a terse, outline-like style, the book presents the history of the Church's involvement in the struggle, interspersing factual accounts with personal observations and quotations from Romero." *NACLA Report*

ISBN 0-88344-019-9   *128pp. Paper $4.95*

THE WORD REMAINS
A Life of Oscar Romero
by James R. Brockman
"It is unlikely that we shall see a better book about Archbishop Romero. Brockman has been thorough in his research. He writes with personal sympathy about Romero and his development within and in response to the unfolding of the Salvadoran tragedy. He is balanced in his judgments and accurate in his reporting of Salvadoran politics, the poverty and the violence which are the framework of this story." *Catholic Herald*
ISBN 0-88344-364-3   *256pp. Paper $12.95*

WITNESSES OF HOPE
The Persecution of Christians in Latin America
edited by Martin Lange & Reinhold Iblacker
Foreword by Karl Rahner
"This book is important because, if understood, it offers a poignant view of the anguished but confident suffering of people who are attempting under great personal risk to live out their faith nonviolently as disciples of Christ. The questions are excruciating, for in so many cases the church has a legacy of close association with those who perpetrate oppression and violence." *Mission Focus*
ISBN 0-88344-759-2   *176pp. Paper $6.95*

GALILEAN JOURNEY
The Mexican-American Promise
by Virgil Elizondo
"Here is a theology that arises from the Mexican-American *mestizaje*. This word must be heard not only by the American Church, but by the Church Universal if we are to incarnate the Word at this time in history. There is no more credible and authentic voice to speak it than Virgil Elizondo. A powerful and moving statement."
Thomas H. Groome, Boston College
"A shining vision of the contribution Mexican-Americans can make to American culture and American life and American religion as they struggle for acceptance and justice and offer, in return, festival and joy."
Andrew M. Greeley
ISBN 0-88344-151-9   *144pp. Paper $6.95*